Fractured Fables:

Twisted Tales

Joe Roland

Contents

A Confrontation   5

Six Characters in Search of an Outlet   9

O'Higgins: His History   13

Noblesse Oblige   17

From The Edge of The Woods   21

Something Wicked   25

Robin Revealed   31

Truth by Tabloid   37

Blood of The Damned   43

A Blast From The Past   51

On the Evils of Drink and Debauchery   57

Much Wurdling   61

Watson Tells All   67

Extracts From The Log of The Bountiful   73

A Hard Knight's Day   79

Lashed by a Writ   85

Judgement Day   99

Winning The Big One   105

A Day in The Life Of...   109

Wapshott's Worst Case   117

Do Not Go Gentle   123

Off The Wall   129

Yonder Peasant   135

Oop at Fahrm   141

The Three Bean Scam   147

The Lonely Grave of Granny McDuff   155

FRACTURED FABLES

A Confrontation

Local Meeting Erupts into Fracas

Scheduled as a convivial meeting of Turtle Meadows Sidewalk, Lawn and Herbaceous Border Watch, the gathering broke up in what one witness described as "savage disarray" when Acting Chairperson, Maude Balfe-Overbearing, suggested that all members in good standing and with paid-up fees were behooved to contribute equally towards some suitably located half-way relief station for "the voiding needs of our four-footed friends." This, Mrs Balfe-Overbearing claimed spiritedly "would preserve the hygiene, bouquet and pristine character of our lanes and by-ways at a relatively insignificant cost." The suggestion immediately raised objections from Member-At-Large Commander R. 'Bob' Bracewattle, R.N. (Ret.) who stated heatedly that, as a well-known and disliked breeder of Irish Wolfhounds Mrs. Balfe-Overbearing had a vested interest in such an undertaking whereas he, with one small Jack Russell of costive disposition, should not be expected to contribute on an equal share basis. It was, the Commander explained, simply a question of quantity versus quality. Following several spirited "here-heres" from owners of the smaller breeds, Mrs. Balfe-Overbearing became increasingly irate, charging that certain malcontent members had obviously conspired to vote against the proposal out of personal bias and that her charges, being well-disciplined in such matters would never, due to superior bloodline, stoop to such anti-social behavior in any case. Fuel was added to the flames by local meat vendor Hal Porterhouse who, when asked for his opinion, said that, personally, the whole matter was purely academic as people rarely purchased meat for their dogs from him, adding wittily that he had no steak in the matter. Visibly stung by these remarks Mrs. Balfe-Overbearing lost composure and struck Porterhouse sharply on the head with a hard-cover edition of 'Stooling and the Modern Dog' from which she had intended to quote at length. The meeting then erupted in partisan shouting as Commander Bracewattle, in a well-intentioned attempt to forestall further mayhem, applied a Half Nelson to Mrs. Balfe-Overbearing who bit his fingers, later claiming self-defense against unprovoked assault and gross indecency. Order was finally restored when building custodian Charles 'Chip' Umbrage, acting in what he considered the best interests of all, turned on the fire alarm and activated the recently installed sprinkler system which he later stated "worked real dandy!" Following these events, saturated members voted an almost unanimous 'No' to the contentious proposal whereupon Mrs. Balfe-Overbearing tendered her resignation and left the hall in high dudgeon wearing a borrowed double-knit cardigan in dark rose. Interviewed later Balfe-Overbearing displayed what she claimed to be deep thumb marks in the upper torso region and said that since the assault she had suffered from stress, sleep deprivation, dizzy periods, loss of composure and problems in wearing normal support garments. Legal suit is rumored pending.

FRACTURED FABLES

Six Characters in Search of an Outlet

1....**Sir Titus Axminster**, a carpet knight who rose to fortune via bankrupt broadloom stock. Sir Titus, Magistrate, Master of Hounds, Seignior of Have-it-All House and its extended bailiwick is keen on all things rural including the wives and daughters of his tenants. He is of choleric bent, an unabashed advocate of hanging, mantraps, public flogging and the repeal of minimum wage laws. His Heraldic Motto, 'Let Them Eat Orts' has not endeared him to the peasantry who mutter incantations for his early demise. He is not popular.

FRACTURED FABLES

2....Doris Wemp-Pilsbury, a fortyish widow with ranking moustaches. Plump through excessive stout drinking, Doris, lately relieved of her fifth husband, is set on becoming Lady Axminster. A consummate snob and social climber she refers to those she deems her inferiors as "the other people." She, too, is not popular.

3.... Denis 'Doughboy' Pilsbury, the immature son of Doris by her first marriage. Doughboy, white-faced and hairless, is of sinister aspect and suspected by locals of having a dubious interest in sheep. He is refused drink in the village pub and often bitten by stray dogs many of which die afterwards frothing at the mouth.

4....Hamish McNutt, gatekeeper to Sir Titus Axminster. McNutt is a retired police informer and aspiring Morris Dancer to which last pursuit he has forfeited the sight of one eye. Dour to the point of mania, he speaks with an impenetrable Scot's accent. Apart from dancing he is socially isolated due to his terrible breath.

5....**Maury 'Mabs' McNutt**, spinster sister of Hamish McNutt, Maury is a religious ecstatic and amateur cloth weaver claiming to be of Druidic descent on her father's side. Often seen rolling nude among nettles and balancing things on her head she is frequently subjected to ridicule and light stoning.

6....**Dirk Whistle**, a silly fellow and unacknowledged son of Sir Titus, Dirk has large red ears, a receding chin and wears a flapping pink cravat. He drives around the countryside in his vintage coupe-de-ville banging into stray cows and running over chickens. Often heard shouting "Tally-ho, there!"

The Plot? Entirely up to you....

FRACTURED FABLES

O'Higgins: His History

The birth of O'Higgins is believed to have taken place sometime in the summer of '29, and the place of his birth to have been Waghampton Railway Station, Parcels. His father was by rumor one of several possibilities including Maurice, the Fifteenth Earl of Waghampton, the name O'Higgins being that of his mother, Ethel Nair O'Higgins, the seldom heard and little known Irish baritone who, later in life astounded her small audience by becoming a basso profundo. The deep-voiced Ethel forfeited an unpromising career by eloping with an alcoholic bassoonist who disappeared immediately after the wedding with the least ugly of three bridesmaids.

Enraged at such an early betrayal, Ethel took refuge in Waghampton Hall where she was engaged to do laundry, darn the earl's hose, and shave him, gaining His Lordship's affection by rendering his favorite hymns and giving him "the best damn lathering I ever had." Following a two-year gestation period after conception O'Higgins was born and, due to a ruptured water main, dry-christened Ethelbert in Waghampton Parish Church. Later, exposed to several weeks of tutoring at the local parish school he emerged a total illiterate with marked anti-social tendencies and early evidence of male-pattern baldness. Entering the workforce he was employed variously as a trainee scarecrow, circus cannonball, and lead blower before retiring on one lung to make his fortune. Penniless at the age of forty-two, he married Mavis Finchwater of no known address. Fortunately, for all concerned, the union did not last more than two weeks, being annulled on the grounds of non-consummation and adultery. When asked by a social counselor what his aspirations were O'Higgins said he didn't understand the question and left swearing vehemently.

Subsequent to these events his police file expanded rapidly, soon holding numerous charges including an unprovoked assault on a fire hydrant towards which he appeared to have developed a severe antipathy. Following this he embarked upon the serial molestation of milk float horses. Described in court as 'short, balding, toothless and vicious with one ear missing' (presumably from horse bite) he was readily identified upon the issue of warrants. No record of military service has been found despite his claims to having served in two world wars and stated desire to serve in a third. Civic offences involve the wearing of a woman's wig and fruit hat for the purpose of getting accepted as a dues paying member of The Daughters of Decency in which venture he was successful before being observed relieving himself from the vertical. His membership revoked, he next joined the Waghampton Temperance Union as banner carrier and door-to-door witness, shortly thereafter being dismissed for indecent exposure and intoxication. His political activities include running as Conservative Candidate for Waghampton West following his claim to be the bastard son of the Fifteenth

FRACTURED FABLES

Earl. Shortly after making his acceptance speech he absconded with party funds, the canteen lady and a twenty pound cheese. The current whereabouts of O'Higgins are unknown. Last rumored to have been seen diving off Waghampton Pier at low tide, a follow-up investigation revealed nothing beyond the discovery of a worn toupee, a set of false teeth and a fouled deck chair. Any information as to O'Higgin's whereabouts would be welcomed by Waghampton's official biographer and the County Constabulary.

FRACTURED FABLES

Noblesse Oblige

The family estate of Sir Humphry Chuff-Withering. It is of relatively modest extent comprising but three or so trout streams, two grouse moors, a couple of lakes and twenty-odd tenant families in various stages of debilitation. Sir Humphrey, who prides himself upon his generosity of spirit, charitable disposition and egalitarian principles is currently engaged in the annual inspection of 'my people' as he likes to call his tenants. Let us join him as he raps with his riding crop on the door of what might well be mistaken for an abandoned chicken coop. The door is slowly dragged open by an ancient crone wearing an apron made from a feed sack. She peers at her visitor with a blank and hostile stare.

Sir Humphrey: (briskly) 'Mornin' Nellie. Is your husband about?

Nellie: (peevishly) About what? He's not up yet is he? He's been at the cider again hasn't he? Besides that, he's right poorly.

Sir Humphrey: Is he by Jove! What seems to be the problem?

Nellie: How should I know? I'm not a doctor. Besides he won't talk to me since he lost his teeth.

Sir Humphrey: Well, I'm afraid he'll have to talk to me. Bailiff tells me the rent's in arrears.

Nellie: Then, you'll have to shout. His ears are waxed up again. It's the damp that does it.

Sir Humphrey: (looking around) H'mmm, perhaps it's the roof. It seems to have holes in it. I'll have Bailiff stuff in some straw.

Nellie: I don't think he'll last much longer, Mister. You should hear him cough. It really makes you sick to listen.

Sir Humphrey: I'd rather not, but perhaps I should take a look. Cheer him up a bit and warn him about the arrears. I'm not a charity you know.

Nellie: You can suit yourself. I've got some chickens to neck in the yard.

Sir Humphrey enters the hut. The floor slopes steeply towards one end which appears to be several inches deep in straw and chicken droppings. At the far corner of the hovel the ceiling has sagged down over a low cot supported by four empty cider kegs. Something stirs beneath what once might have been a blanket.

Sir Humphrey: So! There you are, Ned. I've half a mind to have you tumbled. Nellie says you've been on the cider again. And what's all this about losing your teeth? I won't have my tenants going about toothless. It reflects on me. And stop being sick. I won't have that either. Apart from which I need a spare beater. Grouse season opens tomorrow. So get off your arse and shape up.

Ned props himself on an elbow, coughs horribly, groans and turns his face to the wall.

Sir Humphrey: Don't malinger with me, Ned Firkin. I've seen men falling like flies in my day. All you need is a boot up the arse.

Ned: (lifting his head and groping for a chamber pot) Why don't you bugger off you daft old pratt? You get on my tits!

Sir Humphrey: You'll not talk to me like that, Neddy, lad. Haven't I tried to make you feel wanted? Eased your path through the troubles of life? Given you leftovers from our table and bought you a crutch when you lost your toes? Lifted the burden as it were? Any more of this and you're out on your ear. Do you hear me now?

But Ned has rolled back onto his side. He belches loudly, breaks wind and starts to snore. Sir Humphrey sighs, shakes his head slowly and snaps his riding crop. One does one's best. What can be done with the laboring class?

FRACTURED FABLES

From The Edge of The Woods

Excerpt From a Colonial Diary

This day unto the Lord a rare glimpse of sun above the valley giving to us much gladness of heart as winter has sore oppressed us lately. Perhaps with the advent of more clement weather an amicable spirit may yet invest our small community. And not, it grieves me to relate, a day too soon, much mischief and ill-will having been conceived through the long chill nights of our discontent. How many times have I left my bed at break of day only to find my hen-house violated overnight? My hens, too, I suspect. Or yet another daub of hexes on my kitchen door? There are those about us who harbor small charity to our ways and customs.

FRACTURED FABLES

But, to the day's account:

Aroused at dawn by Goody God-Save-Us-All, my swart house helper who, acting in the stead of my dear companion now departed these many years, arouses me not infrequently. Having broken fast by means of month-old bread I bent to my husbandry digging up the shriveled tubers, the which serve as our daily sup, ignoring as best I could the surly scowls and shouted denigrations issuing forth from passing carts. We are, I sadly fear, removed by more than distance from the harmonies of civil life, surrounded on all sides by inbred brutes bereft of all the Christian virtues. And yet this day I must go forth into their midst for our provender which is running perilous low with little to be procured from the trading post but month-old cakes and moldering sides of odorous pork the like of which laid my good spouse in her early grave. Also I must buy feed for my flock of laying fowl, hard-pressed these several months by lack of corn the most of which I had put to baser use to raise my sinking spirits through the drear season. Much tribulation also I lay at the door of those among us in their obeisance to the Evil One, ever in wait for the frail or fornicated. Also these latter darkened days there has been witness to red eyes glaring from the forest, the gathering of wolves, the sound of fluting with dire forms dancing in the shadows, the rumor of midnight congress by fiends and wenches bereft of shifts and drawers, among them, I fear, my swart wench Goody while I sleep through the dark watches. Dear Lord I fear that we have witching in our midst. And who next among us shall be pressed or put to the iron?

  Lest I be thought uncharitable in these accounts, have thou in mind always the gentle nurturing to which I was accustomed. Not for me the coarse and brutal badinage of rural life, nor yet the pastoral wit of village pranksters to whom the midnight toppling of a privy or the throwing of some simpleton into the village midden are sources of high merriment.

  Eventide again, in the number of our days. As I set the traps about my house to snare the would-be felon and bolt my doors against the midnight fist, I look out over the darkening land and wonder who lurks yonder in the hidden places awaiting the footfall of the unwary. What fell mischief shall we witness yet? And so to my bed at days dark ending to be aroused once more upon the early morrow by my faithful servant Goody who, praise be, will never breathe a word to anyone.

FRACTURED FABLES

Something Wicked

A blasted heath. Blackened and stumpy trees half sunk in pools of stagnant water. Fog and filthy air curl over the barren landscape. Above, dark scudding clouds. A crow croaks dismally and falls to earth with a damp thump. This is not high end real estate. In the foreground three ancient hags maunder over a foul-smelling pot. They are run-of-the-mill witches - crooked noses, warts sprouting hairs, rheumy eyes. When they open their mouths to shriek they reveal their pot-holed dentistry. They are of contentious disposition.

First Witch: Who brung Eye-of-Newt? I didn't. Eye-of-Newt wasn't my responsibility. I've brought Tongue-of-Dog but tell the truth there's not much left. Something had a go at it.

Second Witch: H'mm! Where's my cat, Graymalkin? We could use him at a pinch.

Third Witch: I don't like that. Stick to the original recipes I always say. You can't go wrong with traditional ingredients.

First Witch: Well, what can we do about it? And what did you bring, eh? At least I brought a piece of the right animal.

Third Witch: (huffily) I brought poisoned entrails, didn't I?

Second Witch: I got a nice bit of Goat's Gall this morning. They were nearly sold out.

First Witch: Well, apart from Eye-of-Newt we've got everything else and it says in the book you can always double up on Lizard's Leg. I've got some left over from Friday. Let's do it.

The witches all join hands and shuffle around the pot chanting "Double, double, toil and trouble, fire burn and cauldron bubble…"

First Witch: (muttering) Hang on…it won't work.

Second and Third Witches: (in unison) Why not, sister?

FRACTURED FABLES

First Witch: The bloody fire's gone out hasn't it!

Second Witch: (irritated) Well, don't just stand there like a tit. Kindle it again.

First Witch: I can't. The Lucifers are damp, aren't they? It's all this fog and filthy air, isn't it? I knew we shouldn't be doing spells in this sort of bleeding weather.

Third Witch: Watch your tongue, madam! You sound like a fiddler's bitch.

Second Witch: If you two are going to keep squawking I'm packing it in for the day.

First Witch: Then sod off. Who's keeping you?

Third Witch: Why are we doing this? I mean, just look at us — soaked to our drawers and freezing our bottoms off. What's the point?

First Witch: Have you forgotten already? To meet MacBeth. We have to tell him about The Wood business. It's what we're supposed to do. It's in the plot. We don't have any options. I didn't really want to do this sort of thing. I was keen on getting married, once.

Second Witch: (cackling peevishly) Getting married? Who'd marry a hag like you? Me, it was acting — the smell of the greasepaint, the roar of the crowd. Or was it the other way 'round?

First Witch: (pulling a hair from her nose) Watch your tongue! I've half a mind to give you a good pinch.

Second Witch: (cackling nastily) Just try it, sister. I'll send a rat up your drawers.

The witches continue to bicker among themselves, shuffling half-heartedly around the pot and muttering incantations. Suddenly a frog hops into view and croaks monotonously. This is Paddock.

Third Witch: What's he doing here? He gives me the creeps.

First Witch: Who? I don't see nobody.

Third Witch: (pedantically) Anybody.

First Witch: Airs and graces! We know you were born in a ditch.

Second Witch: I'm all for packing it in. The fire won't light. We can't cast any spells, nobody's coming, plus it's starting to rain again. I vote we just bugger off.

Third Witch: Well, let's do it properly, then. Rules of Order and that stuff.

They all join hands and turning widdershins chant:

> When shall we three meet again?
>
> In thunder, lightning, or in rain?
>
> When the hurly-burly's done,
>
> When the battle's lost and won,
>
> That will be ere the set of sun, etc..etc..etc...

Exeunt to loud thunder claps and other cheap theatricals.

FRACTURED FABLES

~~~~~~

Robin Revealed

Sherwood Forest in the late Eleven Hundreds. It is a dense cluster of tangled oaks and bushes. Overhead, crows caw harshly over a rubbish dump. In a small clearing a gathering of men crouch around a smouldering fire arguing among themselves. Known as Ye Merry Men they are a sullen and villainous assortment of pickpockets, cutthroats and footpads. Several have no trades at all. Rousted from the streets of Nottingham, they owe allegiance to no one but their leader. This is Rob-in-Ye-Hood, known to a few close friends as Bobby. Rob stares gloomily into the greying embers. Defying legend, he is a short, not-to-say squat fellow with shifty eyes and a straggling moustache that has seen better times. He is wearing a moth-eaten William Tell hat, what might once have been a Lincoln-green jerkin, mildewed tights and down-at-heel buskins. He is not a prepossessing figure and owes his leadership to cunning and cheating at cards. His weapon of choice, a sawn-off English longbow is much feared among his men many of whom have suffered collateral damage due to his poor eyesight, lack of training and a failing grade in toxophily. Today, Rob is in a contemplative mood. Raising his gaze from the embers he addresses what is left of Ye Merry Men who now, due to attrition, desertion and hanging, number four only. They are Will Scarlet, a bumbling ex-poacher with gingery hair, Little John, a seven foot lout and quarter staff artist charged with several counts of assault and thuggery, Friar Tuck, a de-frocked monk with, among other indispositions, an eating disorder and high blood-pressure, and Alan a Dale, a tone deaf, would-be folk singer and third-rate lutenist not much liked by the other merry men. Robin raises his head. He has come to a decision:

Robin: It's time to pack it in, lads.

> Ye Merry Men exchange uneasy glances. Pack what in? Do they have options?

Will Scarlet: What's all this about, then, eh?

Robin: This so-called life we're living. If you can call it that. Cold, damp, no decent grub. All the rabbits and pheasants gone God knows where. Nothing to poach. Not even an egg. Just crow pie and hedgehog. I ate a frog yesterday. So nasty!

Little John: I bin chewin' on acorns. They give me the runs.

Robin: (moving away) Don't think we haven't noticed.

Friar Tuck: I'm down to half my usual weight. Still, I saw my thing this morning.

Alan a Dale picks up his lute, hums a few off-key notes, then starts to improvise:

Oh, merry, merry men were we

Singing beneath the Green Wood Tree

With lots of grub and girls for free

One for you and two for me

FRACTURED FABLES

Will Scarlet: Why don't you stuff it you daft pratt! A man with your lack of talent. You couldn't play Three Blind Mice. You should've stuck with your regular job. Swabbing up outhouses wasn't it?

Friar Tuck: Why don't we ask for a pardon? If I could get my stipend back I'd go like a dose of salts! Besides, those boys were lying.

Little John: No they wasn't, mate. I seen you at it.

Robin: Shut up the lot of you. The sheriff would hang us like a bunch of grapes. When did we last stage a decent holdup? Let's face it lads - we're history.

Little John: What about our oath to rob the rich and feed the poor?

Robin: Bugger the poor! They take the money then snitch to the Sheriff. What are we, a charity? No, lads, time to get out. The woods are being developed, trees coming down, row hovels going up and – (Suddenly, Robin pauses) Wait a minute! I just had a thought. No risking our necks staging hold-ups. Just straight B and E. In and out like a fiddler's elbow. It's the same as collecting rent. Better, in fact.

Friar Tuck: But what about the Sheriff?

Robin: I've already thought of that. He's bent as an old boot. We count him in. He gets his and we get ours. I tell you, lads, it's the wave of the future!

Little John: Would I get to use my quarterstaff?

Robin: We're counting on you, Jack.

Alan a Dale: And I could compose some theme music. We could get bookings.

Robin: (fingering his bow) I'll give you a booking if you don't shut up! You're getting on my wick this lately. Now, all of you lads gather your gear together. Were going out burgling tonight...

Unable to contain his muse, Alan bursts into song:
We once robbed the rich and gave to the poor,
With a Hey and a Ho-Nonny-No,
Now Robin's come up with a much better plan and...

But Alan gets no further with his composition as Little John, acknowledging the nod from Robin, deftly quarter-staffs him down from behind.

FRACTURED FABLES

Truth by Tabloid

Dog Talks in Tongues

An Airedale cross owned by Deacon Floyd P. Horlick is no ordinary mutt. Ask any congregant at The Cloud Nine Church of Divine Desperation and they will tell how Ralph rolls on his back when exposed to hymns and howls in several canine tongues. Animal behaviorists called upon to examine Ralph claim to have distinguished Old English Sheepdog, Welsh Border Collie, Alsatian, Pekinese, and French Poodle among many others. One member of the congregation who recently toured the Vatican swears she once heard Ralph bark in Latin. Asked to investigate the phenomenon,

Vaughn Deschiens, the well-known society veterinarian and agnostic, administered a double blindfold test and concluded that in his experience "There's something very weird about this pooch. If he were mine I'd have him exorcised regularly, and neutered this afternoon or sooner if possible."

Struck by Lightning Thirteen Times

Norton Hough, a hotel shift worker was recently struck by lightning for the thirteenth time. Hough who is completely bald from repeated bolts to the head, says it always comes as a surprise and is a still a shocking experience.

"I never know when the next one will hit me," said Hough in a recent interview. Things seem to be going along quite nicely then, whazzam! It's very hard on my nerves."

Hough, who entertains at local charities and fund raisers by screwing flashlight bulbs into his bodily orifices, says the condition is probably hereditary as all his family members have been struck at one time or another, some of them twice in the same day. "We try and treat it as a sort of gift," Hough says gamely.

FRACTURED FABLES

200 Year Old Woman Found in Old Folk's Home

A woman claiming to be 200 years old who says she cannot remember her full name but has no difficulty threading a needle without wearing glasses has been found in a Florida nursing home. Florence X, who claims to have done laundry for Abraham Lincoln up to his death, says that apart from some dizzy spells when she drinks too much at parties she is in "tolerable good health." Asked to what she attributed her amazing longevity, Florence said she didn't quite understand the question but would appreciate a new set of teeth, a pint of Jack Daniels, a Zippo lighter and a carton of non-filter Luckies as she was totally out of smokes.

Tribe of One-Eyed People Found in Jungle

What may be one of the most important events in anthropological history is the finding of a tribe of one-eyed people living in a remote and hitherto unexplored jungle area of the Upper Plate. Discovered by world-renowned explorer/botanist Claude Pith, the tribesmen indicated by universal sign language that they were desperately in need of designer sunglasses, a monocular movie theater and some form of device to prevent their bumping into each other, this latter often leading to bloodshed and fratricide. Pith, who mentioned the discovery during a slide presentation of his collection of leaf caterpillars, was later challenged during the question-and-answer period by enraged explorer/entomologist Weible Bumbeiter who claimed to have discovered the tribe two years earlier. During the ensuing debate as to who had priority Pith's helmet was knocked from his head and several of his specimens trampled underfoot. After the presentation, Pith retaliated by telling a news reporter that Bumbeiter was an uncouth bug grubber of dubious academic standing and wanted in several countries for fraud, currency laundering and numerous moral offences.

Man Recalls Former Life as Circus Elephant

Grant Piffle, a retired transit worker, startled friends and relatives by describing a former existence in which he was a performing circus elephant. Piffle claims he was born in Assam where he was trained to haul logs and later kidnaped by agents of Barnum and Bailey who smuggled him to the U.S. in the hold of a clipper. Asked how it felt to have worked in a world famous circus, Piffle said it was an honor and a privilege but that he had suffered considerably from high blood pressure and irregularity due to a diet of salt peanuts. His former career in show business ended during a street parade in Portland, Oregon when he accidentally sat on the wife of a prominent state senator. Would he look forward to repeating the experience if he were given the opportunity in a future life?

"Most certainly," Piffle affirmed enthusiastically, "I'd pack my trunk immediately."

World Bean Eating Contest Smashed

An unidentified contestant who turned up to challenge the existing champion Jethro Burpee at the Annual Baked Bean Swallow in Mule's End, Arkansas, easily dismissed the competition by forking back twenty five cans of baked beans in less than thirty minutes. Afterwards, while undergoing decompression in the first-aid tent, the man, who refused to disclose his identity, asked only that the feat be recorded in the Guinness Book of World Records and that he be referred to as 'The Lonesome Kid'.

FRACTURED FABLES

Blood Of The Damned

*Outline For A Really Cheap Movie**

Scene 1: Night

Staggering up the dark and twisting track leading to the castle of Count Zhog-The-Unspeakable are a dozen or so villagers (pronounced Willagers) many under the influence of Yertch, an onomatopoeic and sometimes lethal drink distilled from Zherkovian bogweed. In their blackened and pot-holed teeth they grip flaming pitch knots, thus leaving their hands free to pilfer each other's pockets or grasp an assortment of agricultural implements

---

* Blood Of The Damned is set in the year 1850. Not that it matters.

intended for use as weapons. Most of them have opted for pitchforks, sickles or flails and the like although one, more imaginative perhaps, is bent double under the weight of an antique plowshare while another, more inventive, shoulders a hog castrator and is for some unexplained reason, wearing an inverted bed pan on his head. As they approach the great iron gates beyond which Castle Zhog looms menacingly, several of the villagers soil themselves in terror, for are they not standing on the very threshold of the place in which lurks a monster who has terrorized their village for years beyond memory? How many have lost their wives, sisters and daughters, voluntary or otherwise, to Zhog's perverse peculiarities? And who among them has not felt the lash of his crop across their buttocks or suffered the humiliation of having him blow his nose on their smocks? Sheeplike, they turn to the man they have unanimously chosen as their leader. This is Zharko, an enigmatic newcomer to their village who has already impressed them with his ability to armpit their national anthem while tap dancing on one leg. He is, for some strange reason not explained in the script, sporting chest-high spotted bloomers. Wheezing, shuffling and scratching in their infested underwear, the assembled villagers passively await his directions. Zharko dances up to the grim, spiked gates of Castle Zhog, inspects them for rust spots, then turns to the villagers. He appeals to their manhood, their love of country, their pride in being Zherkovian, then asks for volunteers to step forward. His request is met with lowered heads and averted eyes and when he promises that those who first scale the gates will be awarded with the painting contract there is still no response although the unemployment rate in the village has stood at a hundred percent for more than a century. Zharko looks deep into the faces before him thankful that he is at least upwind. He regards their sullen scowls, their missing ears, their toothless gums. He watches as a dropsical ancient with a mop-handle leg, one eye and not much else left drops dead in his tracks. No one notices. Are these not his comrades, his brothers-in-arms, men of the same blood, The Blood of The Damned? Zharko chews broodingly on his moustache. Then, remembering he is clean shaven for the part, abandons the practice. He holds his head between his hands.

God, what a turnout! Small wonder they are known collectively as "Those who Never Wash."

Scene 2: Night

Interior of Castle Zhog. Dank stone walls bearing candles emitting a dull, sulphurous glow. Lightning flickers continuously through the bat-fouled windowpanes which have been bereft of draperies since Zhog's ninth wife disappeared mysteriously after hanging in the buff for several weeks without clothes or makeup. Zhog-The-Unspeakable enters dramatically from a side door. He is tall for a Zherkovian, having reached the height of five-five in a country where, due to a diet consisting mainly of acorns and fungi, few stand higher than the average chimpanzee. Zhog calls for his servant, Dhurko, a bent-over creature with the face of a condemned cheese. "Fetch eat!" Zhog orders. Dhurko exits and returns shortly followed by a swarm of fruit flies. He is carrying a plate holding something that looks like a stamped frog. Zhog eats hungrily then pauses, his right eyebrow arched. "Vhat's happening?" he asks fetching Dhurko a stunning clout to the head. Dhurko grunts and crabs to the window. He sees the mob outside the gates. "Willagers come," he cackles stuffing a stray cockroach into his mangled right ear and chewing vigorously. "Zho!" Zhog hisses. "Vhat foolishness is this?" Looking out over the courtyard he sees the villagers at the gate, many kneeling down and, following Zherkovian tradition, festooning their private parts with strings of garlic. Zhog smiles evilly. An insurrection! Look at them! And that one at the front who thinks he's directing things! Ha! He, Zhog The Unspeakable, will make an example of him. When he has been hanging from his nostrils for a month or so, he'll know who calls the shots. And the rest? A mass impalement perhaps. Or something really nasty. Vhat a jollity!

Scene 3: Still night

Outside the gates of Castle Zhog Zharko is still attempting to embolden the villagers by performing a Zherkovian folk dance in hopes that this may convince them of their glorious heritage and reputation as fearless warriors. This seems to produce deep despair among them as none can remember ever attacking anyone other than a disabled grandparent and even then only from behind. Nevertheless Zharko persists in his effort and brings off a bravura finale consisting of several cartwheels and a somersault that loses some of its panache due to a split in his bloomers. Hiding his embarrassment as best he can he strikes an heroic pose and recites to his audience.

Writer's note: due to the peculiar vulgarity of the Zherkovian language and the inability of their lyricists to grasp the fundamental principles of measure, rhyme or meter, it is virtually impossible to appreciate the complexities of their national muse, described by one eminent critic as "a cacophony of demented and undecipherable grunts, glottals and obscenities."

After singing several rousing choruses with appropriate gestures the boldest of the villagers rush the gates. Both make it to the top but only one manages to clear the crow-stained spikes and drop to the other side while his less fortunate fellow hangs whining in shrill falsetto. The successful intruder scrutinizes the gates professionally and reports to the rest that there is no lock and all they have to do is push. The news is received with much foreboding; this means that there is nothing to stop them from rushing the gate, overpowering the vile Count and doing the routine Zherkovian pointed stick routine before recovering what is left of their wives and daughters and putting the Castle of Count Zhog to the torch. Muttering spreads among the villagers. Is this the wisest course? Aware of the deteriorating situation, Zharko pushes open the gates and marches up the driveway. "Who will follow?" he calls out heroically. To a man they turn and run down the mountainside trampling several of their incapacitated elders underfoot. Zharko pauses and smiles sardonically as they disappear into the night. What did he expect? As he walks up to the castle door to meet the Count himself he smiles sardonically. He's been around. He knows the score. Perhaps he can negotiate.

Scene 4: Still Night

Cancelled...

FRACTURED FABLES

Shortly after reading Scenes 1, 2 and 3 the backers of 'Blood of the Damned' pulled out of production as they felt that what they had initially thought to be a family entertainment was turning into a vehicle for morbid distraction bereft of any of those redeeming social values they had hoped the movie would promote.

They felt particularly that the character of Count Zhog was two-dimensional at best and tended to hold up constitutional authority figures to ridicule and disrepute. Furthermore, the supporting caste, which was to have been presented as pastoral village folk in colorful national costume was simply a parade of grotesques most of whom were depicted as missing essential body parts and suffering from questionable distempers, the whole being totally unsuited to the perceived target audience. Currently the rights to 'Blood of the Damned' are open to purchase. Anyone interested in taking over production is invited to submit a tender via:

    The Official Receiver
    13 Royal Shaft Street
    The City W.1

FRACTURED FABLES

A Blast From The Past

Spoon's the name — Nick Spoon. I'm a private eye but don't ever call me a dick. A guy in my line of business has to have some dignity.

It was one of those days. Outside it was raining again, the kind of rain that gets right into your underwear. I'm not saying things were quiet, but if you held your breath you could hear your dandruff falling. Loopy, my Girl Friday, hadn't been paid since she was twenty-nine again. All my mail had windows and the cash box hadn't been used since last Christmas. Clients were thick as loan sharks at a charity, plus my carpet was worn down to the office below. Another week and I would've been working keyholes. I hate talking like this but it goes with the territory.

FRACTURED FABLES

I lit a cigarette, flipped the match into the wastepaper basket and knocked off the last two fingers of Old Tennis Shoes. I was just on the point of calling it a day when she walked in.

Some dame, I'm telling you. Six foot two with an eye patch. A real looker. She had class written all over her. Some joker with a laundry marker I figured. These days who can tell?

"You're Nick Spoon, aren't you?" she said huskily. I had her figured for a two-pack-a-day dame from the get go.

"That's what it says on the door," I said. I'm pretty quick with a comeback even if I say so myself.

She turned and looked through the window. I couldn't figure this dame at all. It had been boarded up since last Christmas. Some bohunk from bupkis. Suddenly, she wheeled around but went too far. I guess it was the eye patch.

"Mr. Spoon," she gasped. "Where have you gone?"

"I'm right here, sweetheart. Just swing to your left."

"Oh, Mister Spoon, you frightened me. I thought I'd come to the wrong place. I'm desperate, you see. I need your help."

"Who gave you my name, Miss--?"

"Penthouse, Mrs... Please call me Glorious."

"I've never heard it pronounced that way. But O.K. if you say so. How can I help you, Glorious?"

"It's my husband, Squire. He's...disappeared."

Nobody had ever called me Squire. "The name's Nick, Glorious."

She seemed confused. Apart from that we had nothing in common. "Let's start over," I suggested. "It could help."

"You're Nick Spoon, aren't you," she said huskily.

I thought we had established that...

"Mrs Penthouse, do you believe in deja vu?"

Just then to make matters more complicated the Fat Man walked through the door, He could have opened it first. He crossed to my sofa, sat down on himself and overflowed. Where had I seen this card before? I pushed the empty bottle towards him.

"Have a snifter, pal; make it a double and quick."

He laughed. "By gad, sir! I do like a man with a

sense of humor."

"Get to cases, fella," I snapped. Something about the Fat Man was getting to me. His aftershave I decided.

He laughed again. "I also like a man with a mind for business. I see we'll get on famously. Who's the lady."

"If it's any of your nevermind, this is Mrs. Penthouse. You can call her Glorious if she has no objections. She's a client of mine and her husband's taken a powder."

"Disappeared," Glorious said. "Squire would never take a powder. He's always been quite fit."

So that was what the Squire business was about. I catch on pretty quick sometimes. Things were starting to fall into place. Her husband had left home.

The Fat Man folded fingers like a bunch of bruised bananas. "Squire Penthouse the Third? I met him in Shanghai three years ago. I believe he has something of interest to me."

Suddenly the picture started to clear. "The Falcon," I said. "The Maltese Falcon. You're Kaspar Gutman and you're after The Bird!"

The Fat Man gave his short barking laugh. "By

Gad! You are a character, sir, and I do admire a man of character."

I was just starting to figure things out when something hit me from behind. I went down smelling bad aftershave. The floor came up to meet my kisser. It could have tasted better. Just before I passed out cold I saw them going through my drawers. It was Gutman and Glorious, alright. How could I be so dumb? As things went dark I wondered why I'd been set up. Wasn't she supposed to be my client? What was she after? Was Squire Penthouse really her husband? What had Gutman to do with her? What was the payoff? Why was I asking so many questions? I blacked out to some busker on the street below. He was playing 'Jingle Bells'. Some timing! It was the first of April.

I woke up in a dumpster somewhere on South Street. There was a lump on my head the size of a grapefruit and my mouth tasted like a shopping cart handle. Plus it had started to rain. I climbed out the dumpster, walked onto the street and rode a trolley downtown. A white port wine bum was sleeping next to me. I pushed him straight and got off at my stop. A crowd was milling around my building which was lit up like the Fourth of July.

"What happened?" I asked a fellow warming his hands.

"Some dumb bunny started a fire in there. They think it's maybe the dick on the second floor."

Then I remembered the match I'd thrown into my waste basket. Some days nothing works out. This would cost. I'd have to sleep somewhere tonight and I reached for my wallet. I pinched on fluff. Then I remembered the bum sleeping next to me. Some bum! Some detective! Some fire! So, Spoon's the name – Nick Spoon. I'm a private eye but don't ever call me a dick. A guy in my line of business...but you've heard all that before. It's a dirty job and the pay is strictly from peanuts. But... somebody's gotta do it!

FRACTURED FABLES

On The Evils of Drink and Debauchery

A Redemptive Discourse
By The Reverend Floyd P. Chaffee, DD.

The interior of a large circus tent. It is a malodorous assemblage of frayed rope and sagging canvas stained by the passage of time, stray dogs, and things best not looked into. The air within is humid and foul with the fumes of stale popcorn, sweat, and that curdled milk smell common to all structures that have sheltered livestock and the unwashed at some time or other. Wobbling chairs with boot-scarred legs and worn seats have been arranged in ranks of half-circles facing a makeshift rostrum across the skirt of which a hand-written banner enjoins 'Repent, Reform, Rejoice.' On this structure a wobbly lectern has been mounted center stage. The audience numbering perhaps thirty or so layabouts in various degrees of degeneracy is already shifting restlessly and several members have begun shouting ribald comments while one such fellow, imagining himself possessed of comedic abilities, has mounted the rostrum and is lurching back and forth in what he mistakenly imagines is an accomplished feat of terpsichore. Failing any acknowledgment or applause he leaves the stage gaping sheepishly just as the guest speaker appears. The Reverend Floyd P. Chaffee mounts the rostrum. Invited by the Daughters of Divine Fortitude (none of whom is in attendance) he is a gross-bellied figure in musty black suiting that exudes a powerful reek of armpit and Old Swampy. His face, fringed by a moth-eaten beard, is not reassuring. A violently mottled nose and small bilious eyes glaring out from under simian ridges give him the likeness of a demented baboon. He clears his throat, pokes through several well-thumbed tracts, looks up and acknowledges his audience. His oratory is an empurpled hodge-podge of corn-pone evangelism and misquoted scripture. He coughs horribly, hawks into a voluminous red handkerchief and begins:

"Good evening, brethren. I'll preach to you this day on the perils of strong drink and the evils of fornication, both of which vices, I'm told, being rampant among the population hereabouts. Now, when I say drink I am not referring to the reasonable ingestion of a moderate beaker of sassafras as a post prandial of the therapeutic persuasion. Nor am I referring to the customary imbibition of the draft that refreshes but does not intoxicate, namely tea in all its sundry manifestations. No, sirs! That to which I refer is spiritous frumenti, the grain of Beelzebub, the destroyer of homes, orphaner of babes and debaucher of youth, and woe unto them that rise up early in the morning, that they may follow strong drink, etcetera and such. And when I say fornication I am not referring to the connubiality of the lawfully conjoined, so sanctioned in the eyes of the Almighty for the getting of childer and so forth. No, what I refer to is the sin of looking upon your neighbor's wife or daughters. Worse yet upon her husband. Also the noxious and depraved habit of looking upon one's self, this causing the gnashing of teeth and everlasting blindness, etcetera, etcetera. All these being sins of the flesh and unpleasing to The Lord, Hallelujah! Praise be!"

As the Reverend drones on, his audience, unable to comprehend the diatribe, grows bored and irritable and turns to other pursuits, gumming hip flasks, shooting craps, picking pockets and fighting savagely. Amid the growing tumult someone fires a pistol in no particular direction. A dead crow plummets to the floor. Men dash towards the exit flap shouting imprecations. The Reverend, wisely deciding that the meeting is now terminal and seeing no further profit in his staying grabs his bible and carpet bag, crawls out under the rostrum, thence through a gap in the canvas. As he leaves the tumult behind he reflects on the frailties of his fellow men and congratulates himself upon his foresight in taking his fee in advance, The Lord being with him always he believes, working in mysterious ways His wonders to perform, Praise be and Halleluja!

FRACTURED FABLES

~~~~~~~~

Much Wurdling

Extract from an article submitted to and rejected by fifty-seven publications covering Travel, Nature, The Environment, Agriculture, Horticulture, Country Crafts, Animal Husbandry, Legend, Folklore, and Rural Psychoses.

Much-Wurdling-On-The-Damp: This picturesque old hamlet is reached by municipal punt which navigates the surrounding fens each third day excepting Sundays, Wednesdays, Sacrificial Holidays, or during outbreaks of Wurdling Plague. (This rare distemper, endemic to the area and classified as Bog Fever 4 to which local inhabitants appear to have developed immunity, has on occasion proven fatal to outsiders.) The inhabitants, who are noted for their dour disposition, ingrained distrust of strangers, and fratricidal dementia, display clear evidence of a drastically reduced gene pool. An inability to count beyond ten without removing their clogs, ride tricycles, or differentiate between vertical and horizontal, together with chronically loose bowels, curtails most activities requiring calculation, balance, direction or hygiene. The menfolk, who may be distinguished from the womenfolk by virtue of their smaller heads and dependent genitalia have been chronically unemployed since the late thirteen hundreds when a morally outraged bishop closed down their only source of income, a traditional cottage industry producing novelty flyswatters from braided hog pizzles. Now living on minimal state allotments, they spend their time in The Knackered Plowboy drinking and cursing between hurried trips to the communal jakes, a vintage 'tip-board' model recently designated a heritage structure by the National Crust. The womenfolk of Much Wurdling may also be seen going about their daily routines, the which include such activities as Clump Dancing, the study of chicken entrails, and the brewing of a lethal hard cider from duckweed and apple cores (See ref. to Loose Bowels).

FRACTURED FABLES

Village life in Much Wurdling should not, however, be thought of as having no compensations, the inhabitants enjoying many social functions of a richness not often found in urban society. Among the several diversions available is the well-known Wurdling Witch-Pricking Contest, the current champion, Elijah Halefellow, on one occasion having pricked nine witches in the astonishing time of seventeen minutes, a record upheld by Village Council despite objections that Elijah had strayed from accepted rules by not using the customary bodkin. A further diversion engaged in by the community is that of 'Witnessing', an after-hours activity played only by those who have achieved the status of 'Wise Elder' and comprised of two opposing teams, 'Runners' who hide severally in the village doorways with their posterior parts exposed until discovered by 'Catchers' who then call out "we see you!" thereby earning the privilege of administering one dozen hard whacks with their braided hog pizzles. (See reference to Cottage Artifacts and Industries.) Also of note is the annual event of Saint Ulf's Eve, a time of much rejoicing and merriment and the shedding of those inhibitions ordinarily so necessary to the warp, woof and weal of isolated communities. Accompanied by cow bells and the beating of home-made tympani, the villagers turkey step around a sacrificial fire, consigning to the flames first their outer garments and later their soiled, year-old underwear in a communal cleansing process, culminating in full body immersion in what is left of the hard cider. (See reference to Women's Occupations). Thus, in a state of what one anthropologist has wittily termed 'au naturel disgrace' the populace engage in grope congress to shouts of ribald encouragement. (Sociological Note: although the aforementioned activities may prove somewhat distasteful to those of a more conservative disposition it should be borne in mind that the aftermath of the Saint Ulf's Eve celebrations is a revitalizing of the village bloodline, a necessary boost to what in its lack would likely lead to the ultimate extinction of Much Wurdling's already dwindling population.)

Beyond these all-too-brief notes there is little else to tell of life in Much Wurdling other than to concur with Hobb's remark concerning shortness, nastiness, and brutality, etc., observations he is thought to have made following an accidental visit. (Travel Note: Those interested in visiting Much-Wurdling-On-The Damp are strongly advised to take their own drinking water and to avoid all local ciders, cheeses, and particularly the ill-famed Gelding Pie, this latter being a traditional, although somewhat sinister Much Wurdling repast, see reference to The Knackered Plowboy.)

Further reading:

Cordwangling-on-Crouch. Some Perils of Inbreeding by R. Dennis Lupin, B.Anth.

The Feral Hominids of Upper Chuffing - Throwbacks Among Us by Rev. E. Franze Fatool. D.D.

FRACTURED FABLES

Watson Tells All

In the strict interest of truth, I must confess to disliking Holmes from the very first day we met. This may come as a shock to the many who believe that Holmes and I were bosom friends and confidants. As for our working together all those years - Pshaw! Purely symbiotic, rest assured. You see, Holmes, although established as the Great Forensic Detective, was fundamentally ignorant of medical science despite his pretensions to the contrary. True, he was a regular, if tedious, contributor to The Lancet but his knowledge of the subjects he so speciously expounded upon was culled in the main by regular perusals of the more sensational broadsheets. I, of course, though infernally boring, I'm often told, was a qualified medical doctor and a bona-fide graduate of the Vienna School of Medicine. How was it then that Holmes and I joined forces, as it were, when there was scant liking between the two of us? Did I mention symbiosis? One's memory fails to serve, I fear. But to continue, Holmes needed my credentials as a medical doctor simply to further his growing reputation. One has to allow that he was shrewd, deuce take him! And what, you may ask, was my interest in pursuing the acquaintance? To put it in a nutshell, vanity. You see, by my nature I am infernally dull. Indeed, as you know, I am aware that most who meet me at my club excuse themselves from my company as quickly as possible when I start to hold forth. Admittedly the detailed functioning of, say, the nephritic kidney, or the most recent advances in bowel re-sectioning may not be to everyone's taste or interest but hang it all, a chap must speak of that which he knows or not speak at all, as some clever Johnny once said. So now you have my secret and Achilles' heel: hubris. You see my association with Holmes, whose following was international, added great cachet to my club chats. After all, who among them had been in attendance when 'The

Hound Of The Baskervilles' was brought to bay? And who had witnessed the horror of 'The Speckled Band' or the cunning of Moriarti? I tell you I became the center of it all and chaps hung over my chair. Heady stuff for one who by nature is tedious to a turn.

Despite all this, there came a time when being a colleague of The World's Most Famous Sleuth began to pall. Success you see, had gone to Holmes' head, and as time passed he came to see himself as everyone's superior. After-dinner conversations became unbearable, and he was, among other things, a frightful snob. "Ah, Watson," he would say in that high-pitched nasal drone he affected, "if only you could shed yourself of those tedious middle-class values you so obviously inherited from your provincial parents, what intellectual voyages might we not share!"

"Upon my word, Holmes," I would respond (albeit testily, as his constant references to my middle-class parents and their puritanical virtues was becoming frightfully irksome) "we all must follow our inherited codes." To such an apt riposte he would smile sardonically while rolling up the sleeve of his velvet smoking jacket and pumping a half pint of nutmeg extract into his infernal armpit.

"Holmes!" I would cry, "If you continue in your abuse of such substances I can no longer assume responsibility for your medical state or mental composure."

Ignoring my outburst, Holmes would reach for his violin, an instrument for which, I must say, contrary to popular belief, he had neither talent nor aptitude.

"I'm afraid the strings are kiboshed, Holmes." I said stiffly. "You won't get a semi-quiver out of them."

Again, he smiled with that supercilious curve of the lip I had so come to detest. "I believe you mean quaver," he sneered, petulantly breaking the violin across his knee. "You can toss the fiddle onto the fire for all I care. "The coals are low and in any case it's only a second-rate Strad."

As I flung the abused instrument onto the embers, Holmes reached for his foul meerschaum and commenced to smoke it with a mixture that smelled like rotting mutton. Applying a sulfurous Lucifer, he projected a reeking cloud towards me. I coughed wrenchingly as I have a frightful allergy to the stuff, which Holmes well knew.

FRACTURED FABLES

Attempting to contain my growing irritation by following the Christian precept of turning the other cheek, I prefaced my intended response by saying "As you are fully aware, Holmes, I am by nature a man of modest pretensions, who…"

Here he cut me off rudely. "Let's face it, old chap, you have much to be modest about!"

He sucked noisily on his loathsome pipe before continuing "The trouble with you, my dear Watson," he said, pacing the carpet restlessly and trampling on my bunioned foot, "is not so much your lack of insight as your middle-class…"

Holmes hit the floor heavily as I brought my leaded cane down on his head. There was little in the way of blood to clean away as he was of a bloodless disposition, and within minutes he was dissolving rapidly in the vat of acid I had prepared earlier in the basement under his chambers. You see I had been well-prepared for such an occasion. It only remains for me to say that Holmes did not die from a fall off a cliff as reported, nor was he ever resurrected from any such calamity. I, John Watson,

Doctor of Medicine, did for him of my own free will while the balance of my mind was quite undisturbed. In the vulgar parlance of a later age 'He had it coming!' And are there any who, knowing the truth, would think harshly of me? Gentlemen, with a clear conscience I rest my case...

FRACTURED FABLES

Extracts From The Log of The Bountiful

Christmas at Sea

December 23, 1787: Left on the tide from Spithead this day, shipshape and steady. Crew a jolly bunch of lads, it seems. My officers, too: all bent to their duties with a will. Wind in our favor and every anticipation of a most successful voyage. Had our fiddler, Blind O'Hara, strike up 'Naughty Nancy' a favorite of the crew and had issued a double of rum for all except our cabin boy who, having drink taken, is easily compromised by certain of our complement. I then gave the first toast 'Our Ships at Sea' and issued all hands their daily beer, one gallon per. Ship's surgeon somewhat ripe in his cups but jovial withal. Must keep a watchful eye on him as he may be required to splice my piles, always at question on these long ventures. First Officer Master Christian, a man to be watched; smart at his station and like to promotion I'll be bound. Good family, on authority, lawyers and such. Not a seaman on board but will give of his best I warrant. Indeed, a captain could not ask for a stouter complement. Weather stayed kind throughout this day and in the evening arranged for dancing on the deck, our fiddler, Blind O'Hara, striking up a lively jig. Broached another keg and issued doubles for all except those on watch, each man quite splendidly merry. Surgeon already in a state of stupor as is normal, his drawers danced down to his slippers. Fellow seems quite awash in his cups, but all-in-all, as glad a day as I could wish for and one which bodes well for our enterprise. All the people in keen anticipation of Christmas at sea. My lads shall have a merry time, or my name's not William Bligh.

  December 25, 1787. Christmas morning and everyone quite jovial, the very elements seeming to smile on us most cordially. All hands mustered for a Christmas Breakfast and afterwards had chaplain say a special

FRACTURED FABLES

Yuletide prayer, then ordered Quartermaster to issue triples of Jamaica Rum unwatered, followed by beer and three bottles Madeira, per. Gave the toast 'Ourselves, As Who Else Will Care For Us?' All hands then toasted His Royal Majesty after which, beef and biscuits, salt pork and duff, as much as each man wanted. In the evening dancing on deck again to O'Hara's fiddle. Ship's surgeon carried to quarters, his face empurpled, a color hard to countenance. God grant I never fall under his knife when he is in his cups! All hands called to and supplementary rum broached and issued, cabin boy now included. Ship's surgeon, confound the man, back on deck again crawling on all fours and calling loudly for more grog. I fear he may not last the voyage. Most of the lads now laid out in the scuppers while those still conscious sang praises to our country. Retired to my berth quite early as flair up of my piles, devil take them, commenced shortly after I ate of the duff. In all, though, a most commodious day with a fair wind off the coast of old Spain.

December 26, 1787: All hands mustered for thanksgiving prayers which, led by our chaplain in robust voice, was followed by double issue of rum, ditto beer, myself, alone in all the company, abstaining due to further flair-up of my strangled piles. Yet, gave toast for the day: 'A Bloody War and Quick Promotion.' Ship's Surgeon, wig askew, his britches undone, as sorry a sight as I ever beheld, his face and wattles now hued to deepest purple. Ordered him taken below again and bled by ship's carpenter once 'prenticed to the Sawbone's trade, such knowledge soon to be called on personally I'm afeared. Repaired to my cabin and scalded my parts with brimstone and treacle, the which thereof giving scant relief. Now bound for Tenerife where we shall take on more provender plus grog and beer, my bully lads deserving no less, God bless each one and all.

December 27, 1787: Winds freshening: piles worsening, brimstone and treacle notwithstanding. Sent for ship's surgeon without response, himself now fallen prey to the horrors. Must put him ashore at Tenerife and indent for replacement. Laved my parts with saltpeter and tar, a remedy sworn to by ship's powder boy, my nethers thereafter scorching most grievously. Assembled the people for grog this morning and gave toast 'A Willing Soul and

FRACTURED FABLES

Sea Room,' all seeming smart as paint. How well goes this voyage, apart from my piles. With their abatement I would count myself amongst the luckiest of men. A small unpleasantness at dinner this evening, my having to rebuke ship's mate, lately promoted to lieutenant, for dress unbecoming an officer, and had sharp words with all at table. Ship's surgeon face down in his duff his flies awry and personal parts in gross display, a disgrace to his blood and profession. Later had powder boy over the cannon and soundly rope-ended by boson, my piles, I fear, inducing such cholor.

December 28, 1787: Seas heavy all about us this day with winds from the south-west approaching gale force. I fear unless the weather 'bates we shall be hard put to this night. Piles now pinching grievously, more than a man can scarce contain. Surgeon useless with alcoholic convulsions and dare not seek his services. Fortunate for him he is commissioned and related to an admiral else I would have him flogged then cast in irons despite his qualifications, pox take him, or my name's not Bligh.

December 29, 1787: Barometer falling, piles still pinching. Winds now at high gale force. Stayed in my berth throughout the whole morning, my affliction grown too monstrous to be bourne. What under heaven have I done to earn such misery? At four bells in the afternoon being bereft of bona fide surgeon I had recourse to ship's barber who soon arrived with lather and razor the sight of which caused me to swoon. Taste forbids me from further account of my suffering other than to relate I am now much reduced.

December 30, 1787: On deck at first light, somewhat recovered though smarting still. Weather moderating to fair with a steady wind now in our favor. Pleased to hear that surgeon expired sometime during the dark hours and good riddance to him, damn his soul. Later read special burial rites whereat surgeon's body and sundered tripes were consigned to the deep in company with my severed piles, Job's curse upon them both! Arranged for triple toast and had like issues of rum provided for my bully boys then gave Final Toast of The Day: 'Absent Friends and Those at Sea,' as fitting a tribute as ever I heard. A fair wind astern and Ahoy, to Otaheite! This voyage will prosper yet.

FRACTURED FABLES

A Hard Knight's Day

The castle of Tristram Fitze-Urpe, a once gaily bedight knight now in his declining years who has decided to hang up his lance and spend more time with those of his family nearest and dearest to him, his dogs. It is a relatively modest castle for one of his standing and in order to keep the demesne from the clutches of the King's Tax Collector he has been forced to let out several hovels to the local peasantry, their rent being nine tenths of what they can grow plus a touch of nox prima now and then. Although these modest returns fend off foreclosure by the county Duke and keep him in mutton and ale, Sir Tristram is far from happy. His peasants, treacherous and ungrateful as always, continue to starve at an unreasonable rate, his lady wife has ceased being conjugal, the moat has dried up and the castle drains are smelling again. We find Sir Tristram warming his patched hose before a small fire in what was once called The Great Hall, now used to house several of his wife's aging relatives who, to his disgust, regularly soil themselves. He has with him his trusty seneschal, a servant so ancient and bent he appears to have died and dried up. On closer inspection this proves to be true.

Fitze-Urpe (reminiscing): It all sounded fine on vellum and I don't mind admitting I jumped at the chance. But have in mind I was only fourteen at the time. I'd done my paging at Arthur's Court, so when my name came up for knighting I was chuffed no end. Who wouldn't have been? Of course it was only provisional. You had to prove you were of the right stuff and do something noble or chivalrous. You had your choice. Naturally, being young and a fool, I chose both. A big mistake! We drew straws and who got the short one? Me, of course. And what was my lot? A dragon! Now when I say dragon, I don't mean your average worm. This bugger was over forty feet long with jaws like a nightmare! So there I was, still wet behind the ears and throwing down the challenge. Terrified? I was petrified! To tell the truth I wet my chain mail straight off, turned tail and ran like a rabbit. At least I survived. Of course, they held a Round Table with all of them sitting about - a Red Knight, a Green Knight, a Black Knight who sat at a separate table, and a Pink Knight called Reggie. Well, to cut a long story short, I got off light because of my tender age and blue eyes and Sir Reggie who fancied me I think. But it went on record all the same - Dereliction of Duty in the Face of a Dragon. But they never gave me another shot and to tell the truth I didn't give a toss. The whole thing smartened me up no end. Dragons were going out in any case and there weren't many virgins left to rescue. Arthur was finished mucking about at Camelot and Grail Hunting was all the rage. Expeditions all over the place with extra pay for overseas, and knights getting piked by Turks first day they got off the boat. Not bloody likely! I said to myself. So I ducked out right smart. Got a month's compassionate to see my old dad who'd been dead ten years, and when I got back the rest had sailed off to sort out Jerusalem. I played willing to follow and join the lads, but I didn't push it too hard. Just as well. Most of them got the shaft, and those that didn't caught nasty conditions they couldn't get rid of. So I got a home posting and life wasn't too bad - putting down peasants and burning the odd castle. Parties afterwards with wenches on tap. Until I got married, that is. By then of course I was getting on a bit and things were changing all over. Knighting wasn't what it used to be and dragons were almost extinct; virgins as well. Then when Arthur died in '37 things went up the chimney altogether, and "Bartlemus, Bartlemus...!"

Perplexed with what he interprets as disinterest, Sir Tristram applies a turn of the boot to Old Bartlemus's withered rump only to see him topple slowly onto the fire. Gradually, it dawns on him that Bartlemus is dead and may have been so for some considerable time. Already he is starting to curl at the edges. God's wounds! How annoying! Replacement will cost. (Bartlemus hasn't been paid in years.) After poking the ashes absently, Sir Tristram rises, sighs and, calling his hounds, walks out into the damp courtyard. A gray drizzle over the battlements, rooks on the wind. Watching the dogs at stool, a dismal thought comes to him: with Bartlemus gone, who's going to scoop? Sir Tristram groans deep in his chest. Whatever happened to Ye Good Old Days…?

FRACTURED FABLES

Lashed by a Writ

Malloy was just finishing his breakfast when he heard the letter drop. As most of his mail consisted of threats or bills he rarely bothered to read it until several days had passed, sometimes weeks, if at all. But there was a difference to the sound this morning and after mopping the egg off his chin with a corner of the tablecloth he went into the hallway. The letter lay as though dropped by a designing hand. He stooped, picked it up, though somewhat gingerly, and yawning, returned to the table, flicking a corner of the envelope with his forefinger. Heavy stock, expensive. He worked a yoke-stained thumb under the flap, opened the envelope and took out the

FRACTURED FABLES

letter. The address had a vaguely familiar ring:

> 10, Haughty Court
>
> Top Hole Mews
>
> The City
>
> Attention of P.T. Malloy, Esquire:
> Sir,

I write to you concerning your inexcusable behavior at the reception recently given by myself to celebrate the opening of my lady wife's latest exhibition at The Do-Dada Gallery in Chelsea.

Bad enough the disturbance at the gallery. But why, having turned up (uninvited, I might add) at my place of residence afterwards, and obviously the worse for drink, did you, upon being mistakenly admitted with bogus credentials find it necessary to shout loudly "What's she exhibiting she hasn't exhibited before?"

Such lewd and suggestive comments have no place within my home. Why, at least, could you not have gone quietly to the refreshment buffet and helped yourself to the cold cuts, renowned cheeses, and imported lagers? (Which you shortly did in any case, though neither quietly nor discreetly.)

    Furthermore, your so-called 'sponsor' Mr. Omphalos M'Doudou of The East Kazoo Arts and Cultural Commission, turned out to be totally bogus - a persona no doubt fabricated on the spur of the moment in order to gain access to my table and attendant comestibles. A subsequent check on the various embassies and consulates confirmed our suspicions that no one of that name or office exists. Neither were we able to locate 'East Kazoo' on any map.

    I would also like to bring to your notice the wanton damage inflicted by you to the second-floor bathroom fittings during your bizarre, hour-long occupation of that facility. How anyone in the course of normal ablutions could possibly crack the toilet bowl and leave footprints six feet up the flock wallpaper is utterly beyond one's comprehension. Further, your aggressive and unqualified assertions that these phenomena were the result of hitherto unsuspected subsidence in the area are too absurd to consider. Not only was this irresponsibly destructive of property, it was also embarrassing and inconvenient to our legitimately invited guests, some of whom were forced by nature and the volume of traffic to visit the facility of our neighbor with whom we are no longer on speaking terms. And was it absolutely essential that you added further insult by spraying 'Philistines' in my shaving cream across the bathroom mirror? To which Philistines were you referring? Surely not my wife and self who both have been unstinting in our support of the arts, particularly since we have only lately started to make a modest profit.

Do not think that these matters will remain unaddressed or that you will not be brought to account for them or other grievous offences too numerous to mention. Already my legal advisers have been instructed to bring suit against you following disclosure of your real name and current address by a person who shall remain anonymous. Additionally, several of my guests are considering taking action, particularly those unfortunate enough to have been in your line of fire when you started flinging ham rolls and bottled beers to someone, no doubt a co-conspirator, lurking in the rhododendrons outside our kitchen window.

    Furthermore, after your third and final ejection it was discovered that none of the special stock lager remained and that the towel you wrapped about your head in an attempt to gain yet another entry by posing as a visiting foreign dignitary was found to have been stolen from our ensuite. Also, and to me the most offensive of the many improprieties inflicted by you upon my household, your leering familiarity with my wife and the several other ladies present did not go unobserved nor shall it go unpunished if there is redress under law for such behavior.

    In conclusion, be aware that you will shortly be receiving communications from those parties retained by me and others to bring these matters before the appropriate authorities.

    Yours in Outrage,

    Col. R. Wilberforce de Witte,

    O.B.E (Mentioned in Dispatches)

    Post Scriptum: Should you find it in yourself to offer my wife and self a suitable apology together with a sum of monetary compensation sufficient to cover all damages (list herewith) I am willing to settle these matters out of court. Do, sir, be decent.

    R.W.d'W.

Malloy sat down carefully on his moldering couch and re-read the letter. For several minutes he stared reflectively at his carpet slippers through the ends of which the malformed outcrops of his yellow toenails protruded. He had to reply of course, a question of personal honor. He returned to the breakfast table, brushed away the crumbs and began his response.

    Gandering House
    The Undercut
    Neck End
    Attention of Outraged....
    Dear Sir,

In response to your shrill and hysterical communication lately received by myself, I would like to make the following comments:

    How dare you allege that I attended your wife's recent soiree uninvited? Do you really believe that a person of my standing and reputation would stoop to sneaking into a private conviviality with the intent of illicitly procuring attendant comestibles? Provender which, despite your pretentious description thereof as "cold cuts, renowned cheeses, and imported lagers" turned out to be little other than second rate deli fare resurrected from the showing earlier. As for the imported beers, imported from where, one may legitimately ask? And should you require proof as to whether or not I was invited to the gala event, this is readily to hand and can be made available whenever and if required, the missive in question having been posted to my address and signed 'Mimi d'Amor', a singularly ridiculous appellation in my opinion and probably fictional to boot. Moreover, the assertion that my introductory bona fides are open to question may quickly be dismissed by referring to any compendium of note wherein my authenticity may be verified beyond dispute. And the charge that I invaded and occupied your second floor bathroom for an extended period of time hardly warrants attention. As to your guests being forced to relieve themselves at your estranged neighbor's facility when they could quite readily have eased themselves by using your ensuite, I can only say that no legal authority would countenance such an argumentum ad absurdum. The fact that you single out my so-called inexcusable behavior when more than one of your "legitimately" invited guests could be observed shamelessly voiding themselves off your balcony is testimony to the bankruptcy of your complaints, not to mention the company you choose to keep.

Still further, your casting aspersions upon the existence of my close friend and confident Sir Omphalos M'Dhou-dhou (please note correct status and spelling) of East Kazoo may cause him to bring suit against you for defamation and denial. Following appraisal, Sir Omphalos has indicated his keen distress in this matter and has, in consequence, instructed his secretary, Mr. Kenji Umslopogus to inform you that if you were ever to set foot in their country he could not guarantee your safety among his fellow Kazooans who hold his vision and leadership in high regard.

Now, to the claim you make regarding damages to

your property, specifically those said to have been inflicted by myself upon your bathroom fixtures. A toilet bowl that cannot withstand a modest temblor without concurrent fracture is hardly worth having installed. I suggest that you take issue with the suppliers and demand that they honor their warranties forthwith. To continue, your statement concerning boot prints six feet up the wallpaper leaves me more than puzzled. I distinctly recall removing my boots as a courtesy shortly after entering the amenity as I intended to mount the toilet seat in order to check for hidden cameras in the ceiling, a precaution I have taken for many years now when using unfamiliar conveniences following a distressing case of misidentification. Again, I would suggest that you cross examine your other guests or, failing that, call in a forensic psychic. It could be that your toilet is possessed and overdue for exorcism. Also, sanitizing. Furthermore, the charges of a co-conspirator operating in concert with me to divest you of your special stock lager can only be put down to paranoia or dementia. The ham rolls (if it was ham), all stale I might add, which I tossed out of the kitchen window were meant for the rottweilers

FRACTURED FABLES

I noticed patrolling your so-called garden. Having a great fondness for the more vigorous canine breeds I was simply indulging a charitable and humane urge to boost their calorific intake as they all appeared to be on the ribby side not to mention malnourished. Regarding the few bottles, reported by you as having been flung through the dining-room window, they were in fact empties I was attempting to dispose of as several of the guests were engaged in heated discussions of the various art forms, and the threat of violence was obviously growing. Having first hand experience of the lethality of air-born bottles you should thank rather than condemn me for taking such a prudent and responsible course of action.

A third and final ejection? A towel about my head? It would appear to me that you must suffer from some form of involuntary hallucination. On the night in question I did indeed wear a towel about my head. This was my own towel and had been brought for wearing at selective intervals during the event as a gesture of respect to Sir Omphalos. Might I suggest that you consider a thorough check-up with a qualified therapist, preferably of the

Jungian School and persuasion?

Finally, concerning your remarks about my leering familiarity with your wife and other ladies present. If you must know, it was they who were doing the leering. I have no wish to sow the seeds of discontent or discord within the bosom of your family or among your dubious social contacts, nor do I seek to cast aspersions upon the fidelity of your lady guests but, frankly, if I were you I would stay alert at all times and demand the truth of them.

Trusting that these matters will now be laid to rest without further unpleasantness or costly resort to legal interference, I remain yours in good standing, etcetera, etcetera...

P.T. Malloy, Matriculated.

Post Scriptum (as you so pompously have it) On the day following your gathering, a seismic report was issued by the Ministry of the Environment stating that numerous cases of severe subsidence occurred in several parts of the city, some of them having their epicenter quite close to where your residence is situated. The report went on to say that although damage was slight and no injuries oc-

FRACTURED FABLES

curred, several households suffered cracked ceiling plaster, window panes and toilet bowls.

P.P.S Concerning your gratuitous display of rank, I would inform you that my father was a much-admired and respected first bassoon in The London Philharmonic Orchestra, and a life-long Honorary Member of The Royal Automobile Club.   P.T.M.

And a Writ Received

FUTTOCK, DINGLE & FINSTRAP
Attorneys-At-Law
Notaries Public
Oaths & Imprecations Recorded
Attn: P.T. Malloy, Esq.

5 Malfeasance Chambers,
Tort Street
The City
As of This Day

FRACTURED FABLES

Dear Sir,

Our client, Col. R. Wilberforce de Witte has retained us to act in his behalf with regard to certain incidents which allegedly took place at his residence, namely, Number 10 Haughty Court, Top Hole Mews on the night of August 9 this year. Col. de Witte who communicated with you shortly after the incidents took place and made known his concerns, distress and displeasure, and to whom you replied shortly thereafter, wishes us to issue a writ, forthwith. We are privy to the response you made and have duly noted its irrelevant, fatuous and obviously fabricated nature which, in our professional opinion, is little short of piffle and puff comprised of nothing other than cynical and fatuous insults to our client, a gentleman, scholar, and senior officer in the ranks of our historically triumphant military establishment. Do, sir, be decent. Colonel Wilberforce de Witte and his lady wife, Pansy Maude, both, have been occasioned considerable distress over this sordid affair, so much so that they are advised by their several physicians to take an extended vacation in the Bahamas or Capri, whichever is the more expensive, in order to regain their equilibrium and joie de vivre. It goes without saying that the costs incurred are to be levied to your account and against your assets when the case is settled in their favor and they have recovered their mental and physical health. However, should you, yourself, require any legal assistance in these matters we obviously cannot be engaged, but urge you to seek representation by our non-fiduciary associates Rheinhardt, Goering and Krappenschnapper with whom we have good filial associations and professional accord. If you wish to take advantage of this no more than courteous interest in your upcoming lawsuit, please do not hesitate to contact us so that we may insure your getting a fair hearing in what is likely to be a difficult, expensive and embarrassing procedure. Be aware, you are behooved.

    Yours in Jurisprudence,

    Darcy Dingle
    for Futtock, Dingle and Finstrap Incorporated.

FRACTURED FABLES

~~~~~~

Judgement Day

Early morning in the Court of No Appeal, a narrow, ill-lit kennel whose ceilings are lost in cobwebs and shadows. In the subterranean gloom dim figures scuttle back and forth shuffling papers and nudging chairs. At intervals they cough drily. Above the magistrate's bench hangs a tarnished coat of arms (or legs - nobody has ever looked close enough to verify which) bearing the ancient caution 'Bacon's Not The Only Thing That's Cured By Hanging From A String.'

First in the dock to answer charges is Charles Emerson Twilly, a disgraced and discredited Notary Public referred to locally as 'Pale Ale Charlie.' He brings to court a history of petty villainy including drunkenness, public disturbance, vagrancy, vandalism, leering, loitering with intent, bearing false witness while testifying under oath, affecting a cork leg in public for personal gain and profit, and violating a church pew. Withal, he is a jaunty figure in his late seventies who, leaning on a purloined blackthorn, might easily pass for a man twice his age. His dress, selectively pilfered from the better-priced thrift stores is of an earlier, not-to-say antique cut and for this, his forty-fifth appearance in court, he has chosen an outsize pink herringbone with gangster lapels, a green bowler hat with several dents and an operatic cummerbund somewhat the worse for soup. Thus attired, he peers around the courtroom with the child-like innocence that has served him so well throughout his absconding youth, misspent middle age and unrepentant dotage. The attending magistrate, 'Ten Years Hardnails,' a judge well-known among defense counsels for the apportioning of sentences based upon the severity of his hemorrhoids is in a particularly petulant mood this morning owing to a tainted breakfast kipper and some gloomy forecasts from his attending proctologist. Within the past twenty-four hours he has handed down maximums on numerous cases including one of Johnny Walker's Red Label now safely under lock and key in the Police Benevolent Club.

Dispensing with formalities (he has entered court in his dressing gown and carpet slippers) the first case gets under way:

Magistrate: (groaning) Good Grief! It's you again!

Charlie: In the flesh, Your Worship, and before we commence may I say in all sincerity that you are looking the very picture of impartial jurisprudence.

Magistrate: Really! Don't try to flatter me you old fraud. Do you think for one moment that this court will be influenced by gratuitous appeals to my vanity?

Charlie: Harsh words, Your Worship.

Magistrate: You think so? Just wait until you're sentenced. I'm sick and tired of seeing you in my court. How many times is it now?

Charlie: To tell the truth, Your Worship, I forget exactly. But it's always been a pleasure.

Magistrate: (rubbing his eyes) Where are you living now?

Charlie: The very same place, Your Worship. In a manner of speaking, that is.

Magistrate: What manner would that be?

Charlie: Well, they've cut off the bleeding light, haven't they? And the water as well. Plus they've locked me out.

Magistrate: Then how can you live there?

Charlie: That's just it, isn't it? You've hit the nail right on the head, Your Worship. It's very trying in the circumstances.

Magistrate: (wearily) Will the Clerk Of The Court read the charges...

C.O.C: (coughing officiously) Accused was apprehended after loud singing in a public place, Your Worship.

Magistrate: That's not an offense. Which public place would that be?

C.O.C: The Central Reference Library, Religious Studies, Your Worship.

Magistrate: And what was the nature of this so-called singing?

FRACTURED FABLES

C.O.C: Off-key and obscene according to witnesses.

Charlie: (indignantly) Begging Your Worship's indulgence, it may have been a bit off color but it certainly wasn't off-key. I had the training as a boy - Scales, Solfeggio, the lot.

Magistrate: What in heaven's name were you singing?

Charlie: That's very close, Your Worship - 'Jerusalem' as a matter of fact.

Magistrate: H'mmm! Had you by any chance been drinking prior to your performance?

Charlie: Just a touch, Your Worship. Being cut off from my utilities I was a bit on edge.

Magistrate: (turning to the C.O.C.) What's on the slate, Ernie?

C.O.C: Chief librarian claims defendant was in an advanced state of inebriation and when asked to desist said he would cut out the tripes of anyone who touched him.

Magistrate: Indeed! Was defendant armed in any manner?

C.O.C: Witnesses say he was brandishing a pint bottle of Guinness Stout at the time, Your Worship.

Magistrate: (addressing Charlie) And were you asked to desist?

Charlie: It's a free country, isn't it?

Magistrate: Probably not for the next thirty days it isn't!

Charlie: (indignantly) Thirty days! What kind of a sentence is that?

Magistrate: The kind you're most likely getting.

Charlie: It's winter out there. Don't be so bloody stingy!

Magistrate: And another thirty days for contempt.

Charlie: (relieved) God bless you, Your Honor! I knew you'd come through.

As Charlie is led off to cells he attempts to whistle a spirited version of 'When It's Springtime In The Rockies' but due to having lost both dental plates it sounds much like 'Jerusalem'...

FRACTURED FABLES

Winning The Big One

Zoom in on the set of WHOOP-O-WINNER'S LOTTERY. As a lucky contestant steps up to receive the BIG ONE a blast of organ music reverberates through the studio. The show's M.C. and compere, smiling maniacally, seizes the winning contestant's hand and flings an embracing arm around his shoulders. Lights flash, the theater organ bellows again. The M.C. brays:

"Here he is, folks! This week's lucky Whoop-O-Winner, Mr. Ted Lamprey!" He consults a cue card. "Ted, who is currently unemployed, the father of six children, with no prospects and deeply depressed until now has just been declared winner of The Ten Million Dollar Jackpot. Ted says he bought the ticket on impulse using money he borrowed from his ailing mother's purse just prior to the closedown. So tell us, Ted, How long have you been a player?"

"This was my first time."

"You really mean you never played before?"

"I always thought the odds were stacked against a guy like me."

"Holy Cow! That's just incredible! So how did you feel when you heard the great news?"

"Vindictive, I'd say."

"Hey! Pardon me. Am I hearing you right?"

"You got it, Jack."

"But don't you feel...elated?"

"Well, yes I do. It stands to reason, doesn't it? But deep down I've always felt vindictive. Now I'm filthy, stinking rich I can come out of the closet. No more Mister Nice Guy."

"Really? But won't this make a huge difference to your life?"

"Are you joking? As soon as I heard the news I became unrecognizable. My mother walked right past me on the street."

"You're kidding us! But what will you do with the money? I mean - ten million! The Big Banana!"

"Well, not that it's any of your business but for starters I'll be moving my mother into another house."

"Hey! that's nice to hear. I'll bet she's thrilled to bits. A brand new house!"

"No, she isn't. And I didn't say new house. I'm moving her into an older, smaller one. The missus and I are taking over her place which is much bigger and in a nicer neighborhood than ours."

"But... that's preposterous! Why?"

"Because my mother's a pain in the ass."

"Well, I must say, Mr. Lamprey, you're our most extraordinary winner to date."

"Listen, I haven't even started yet. Once I get the hang of being filthy, rotten, stinking rich I'm going to get really obnoxious."

"You are? Well, well, well! Here's your cheque, then, Mister Nasty Pants. Enjoy."

"You betcha, Jack!" (Contestant snatches prize

money then exits).

The compere holds his hands out. "O.K. O.K. O.K. folks. Some nice guy, eh? I kid you not! But just remember, (final blast of organ) - it's a wunnerful life and you see 'em all on...THE WHO-O-O-O-P-O-WINNERS' SHOW.

FRACTURED FABLES

A Day in The Life of...

Monday again (good grief!). Up far too early this morning, due, I shouldn't wonder, to the roast of pork loin Margaret didn't quite cook for Sunday dinner. Touchy stuff pork as I've often told her. Alas to no avail.

Raining again of course. Disappointing, most, the weatherman having guaranteed a day of brilliant sunshine with cloudless skies. Obviously a fool or a rank amateur. I would 'phone in and complain but time is of the essence. I had planned a day in the garden forking over duff and poking in the odd seed potato. A little late in the season I suppose, but better than never I always say. Unlike the chap next door, who put his in two months ago. All washed out, I'm happy to say. Hours wasted and serve him right. Never took to the fellow anyhow.

    Rather a dismal start to the day. Both cats terribly sick. I distinctly recall warning Margaret not to give them any of the left-over pork. Margaret, herself, quite snappy at breakfast, due, no doubt, to my faux pas at the dinner table last night when we had the Mandibles over for our customary Sunday dinner. Mrs. Mandible was visibly upset about the Cucumber au Vinaigrette I accidently tipped down her front. Drink of any sort seems to affect my sense of balance these days. Attempted to smooth things out with a story or two. My joke about the prelate and his penitential shirt seemed not altogether inappropriate, if a touch risque. Mandible, whom I thought more cosmopolitan, was dreadfully put out although his wife laughed rather coarsely I noticed. How was I to know his brother was a de-frocked bishop? Didn't care much for their overweight child either. Screaming as though she had been bitten by something under the table. She pinched me first I believe. I shouldn't wonder if the Mandibles weren't up and about quite early, too. Must get Margaret to toss out the pork, ptomaine being much on my mind since the early hours.

Things settling down a bit by lunchtime. Nothing to distract me except the goldfish floating upside down. Can't blame the pork for that I suppose, although I wondered at the time if it was wise. Margaret will be quite upset no doubt as she had named it after her mother. Life's full of mistakes though, as I well know.

Perhaps I can blame it on the cat.

Wrote yet another letter to Great Uncle Hodge who seems to be getting quite testy of late. No reply to my fourth letter requesting a small advance repayable some time in the future at current interest rate. To no avail it would appear. Probably hasn't forgiven my referring to him as a stingy old duff on his last birthday celebration. I never thought his hearing was so sharp. Ninety-seven and ears like a bull elephant. No doubt he expects to live forever and probably will just out of spite I shouldn't wonder.

Dashed off a line or so to Op. Ed. Concerning littering and the general public. Lost patience with it and tore the sheet into little pieces then tossed them out the window as a case in point. They never publish my letters anyway so why tilt at windmills? It doesn't do to take life too seriously. Some days, though, I could cut my throat!

Took a stroll in the garden after lunch and returned soaked to the skin. Tackled accounts in earnest - bills, bills, bills. I'm sick of the sight of them. Everyone's hand under my nose or in my wallet. Talk about free lunches! Why can't I get one occasionally? Some very disturbing news in the mail: an aunt of Margaret's threatening to visit us. Says she'd like to stay a month or even longer, perhaps, depending on the weather. A very large and rancorous woman: great bulging calves and outsize tennis shoes, Neanderthal jaw and speckled teeth just like a horse. She took me to task the first time we met, suggesting that I get a haircut and shave off the moustache I had been cultivating. I was doing my very best to impress her, wearing my yellow cravat with the riding crop motifs and pretending expertise in cocker spaniels as she had three or four, all of them sniffing me at once, one even going on my best flannels. Perhaps this time I could put her off by warning of a local outbreak of something - distemper or the hydrophobia, but Margaret would soon find out.

Went to the library in the afternoon and was dreadfully humiliated. Requested Bronsky's 'Sex Life of the Midnight Toad,' an amphibian I have long admired and studied. Assistant said it wasn't in stock as librarian didn't approve of toads, or sex. Situation quickly getting out of hand when I insisted that as salaried public servants librarians had a duty to be familiar with both. Brief shouting match ensued and I was roughly ejected by custodian. May write to the chief librarian, a cousin of mine, though several places removed.

Suppertime and Margaret back with several ladies from her quilting society, all expecting to be fed of course. Am I running a soup kitchen? Not much for supper except the left-over pork, which Margaret turned and dressed with parsley. Bit risky I supposed but waste not want not she always says. Personally, I wouldn't touch it without gloves on. Decided to dine out. Thank God for The Leg O' Mutton!

FRACTURED FABLES

Not too many in the bar, Mondays always being quiet. Still, it gave me time to reflect. Not that I'm dissatisfied with life. Just sick to death of people, particularly the neighbors. Take the Caraways for instance. Always seedy, always complaining. I've never heard of half the things they suffer from. But try to talk about my back condition and they just keep interrupting. I'm sick to death with her bunions. And what do I care about his hemorrhoids, falling or otherwise? They make me sick to my stomach. And then there's the Orpingtons with their silly privacy screen (which I can see over from our bedroom window). Sun bathing in the altogether. I call them the Buff-Orpingtons but Margaret isn't amused as she doesn't see the point of puns. Some people have no sense of humor. Got home rather late but Margaret out. Left a note on the kitchen table saying her boss had called asking her to put in extra time by accompanying him to a midnight drive-in movie, a business he is considering getting into. Nothing wrong with that, I suppose. I admire a man who's got his eye on things. Always stands me a drink when we meet in the pub. I know he thinks highly of Margaret. Nothing wrong with that either. Still, it's probably a good thing she wears horn-rimmed glasses, if you get my drift. And she's lucky I'm so trusting. But who'd get ideas about Margaret these days? I know I don't.

FRACTURED FABLES

Wapshott's Worst Case

When Cockfoster's wife left him and his dwindling circle of friends ducked into doorways to avoid further loan requests, he decided to lower his literary sights. His failure to interest a publisher in his coffee-table book 'Plague Pits Of Old London' had convinced him to try his hand at some form more to the general public's choice. What, he asked me, did I think he best might do? Try the pulps, I advised him - detective fiction, thrillers, true romance - that sort of stuff. He looked at me thoughtfully for a minute before speaking. Detective fiction, eh? Well, yes, he might try that. But what kind was selling? The old standbys, I told him. You know - Sherlock, Poirot, Miss Marples, - sleuths with a touch of the eccentric. He put on his dark glasses and headed for the door. "Really?" he said walking into the wall. "Then that's what I shall do."

A week later Cockfoster was back. He dropped off an outline and three chapters of a work in progress and a request that I meet him for lunch the following day. Perhaps I would prepare a critique of his efforts as he needed some assurance before continuing.

After he left I opened the folder he had given to me. Perhaps he had hit upon something. I began to read:

Wapshott's Worst Case
By Irving Cockfoster

Episode 1. An Alarm at Midnight

The night was warm and wind-torn with ragged clouds veiling the face of a gibbous moon that was perhaps not entirely gibbous but more or less so. High above the dark and ivied walls of Wapshott Hall a flag bearing the ancient arms of the Wapshotts flapped fitfully, while all about the surrounding countryside brooded in a silence so deep it seemed almost palpable. (*Author's query: Am I achieving the right atmosphere of menace?*)

In an upper chamber of the hall a light shone, although somewhat dimly, and by its flickering illumination could be seen a solitary figure made the more so by the absence of any other. Who could be awake at this dismal hour? Lord Henry Wapshott, Special Consultant to The Yard, was hard at work as usual. (*Historical Note: It should be mentioned here that the Wapshott motto 'Let Them Eat Orts' had caused some ill-will among the lower classes within his purview who had on several occasions attempted to present partitions only to find themselves set upon by the much-feared Wapshott hounds.*)

'Wappers' as Lord Wapshott was unaffectionately known among those within his demesne was working late into the night on two of his current books: 'The Thumbscrew As Deterrence,' and 'Poisonous Custards of the Punjab.' Little did he know that at that very moment a dark and turbaned figure, afloat on an inflated sheep bladder was propelling itself across the murky, frog-filled moat. (*Alternatively, the turbaned figure could be creeping in bare-foot stealth across the drawbridge towards the hall's Great Door. What do you think?*)

Wearily, Lord Wapshott lay aside his pen and buried his nose in the box of baking powder ever at his elbow. Quickly enlivened by this ancient folk remedy he cast about the room with his piercing right eye, its sister orb having been plucked out by Abdul The Damned one terrible night in Istanbul (*formally known as Constantinople*). Suddenly, as if in echo of that terrible event, his left ear was pierced by a blood-curdling scream (its brother orifice having been sealed with hot ghee by Akbar The Unmentionable one other terrible night in Peshawar. (*Query possible name change*).

Ever alert, Lord Wapshott reached for the speaking tube at his elbow (*Note use of period technology*) and hailing the servants' quarters, was answered by his trusty retainer, Old Worthington E.

"Yus, M'Lud?"

"Great Scott, Old Worthington E. Who made that bloodcurdling scream?"

"It's Mrs. 'Addock, M'Lud."

"Then box her ears and tell her she's fired again. The mutton was awful."

"Beg pardon M'Lud, it's too late."

"Too late? Too late for what?"

"Mrs. 'Addock's 'ad it."

"Impossible! Mrs. Haddock's a church-going lady. She wouldn't dream of it."

"It's not that, M'Lud. You don't understand. She's been pinned to the pastry board."

"Pinned, you say. With what?"

"A toasting fork it seems."

"Great Scott! The old toasting fork trick! With a message, of course?"

"I'm afraid not this time, M'Lud."

"No message, you say? That in itself could be the message. Check all doors and windows. Top up the moat. You could be next, Old Worthington E.!"

"Yes, m'Lud. If you say so. Will I send for a Bobby?"

"No time for those chaps. This calls for brains and resourcefulness. It could be an agent of Suleyman The Unspeakable or even, perish the thought, Abdul The Awful. Sharp about it now! Pack my tropicals and prophylactics. Forewarned is forearmed. We leave at first light by packet for the continent, thence to Peshawar by way of Rawalpindi, thereafter…"

(*To be continued*)

I picked up my red felt pen and wrote beneath: This work pulses with promise. Graphic descriptions and mounting tension kept me glued to the pages. Include more detail and you could have a winner. Ascend the Mount!

What else could I say to a man who had stood me drink when I, too, was struggling?

FRACTURED FABLES

Do Not Go Gentle

At last you're free! Free to deal with the rest of your life as you please. H'mmm...Really?

For several mornings following your official retirement you wake up, stare at the ceiling and say to yourself: "Good grief, I'm late!" Then you remember and say "I'm not - I'm retired." It feels quite strange. Get used to it. Remind yourself to be on guard. Don't talk about it. Friends (if you have any left) and others also recently retired will expect you to talk to them about it all the time. Resist strenuously. If necessary, divert them with obscure facts. Say, for example: "Do you know that it takes a man falling into deep water while wearing a genuine Harris Tweed overcoat three times as long to drown as another man wearing a cheap herringbone?" Stuff like that. Soon, they won't even want to say "Good morning" to you.

Above all do not join a 'Senior's Support Group.' There you will meet other retirees who will offer you advice and talk about group outings and visits to places of no interest. This will age you rapidly. They will also tell you not to lie in bed late or sit in the kitchen drinking coffee and reading Dagwood Bumstead. They will warn you against not shaving or forgetting to put on your trousers until mid-day. In short, they will tell you not to stop doing all those things you've had to do every morning for forty years. Listen to them and yours is not an enviable future. Among the things they say you should do is "get out into the garden," a therapeutic exercise requiring you to poke around among slug infested lettuce, pluck endlessly at weeds or fix up old rakes with bits of chicken wire while you hum 'Greensleeves.' They will also suggest that you keep abreast of current affairs while thinking positively. A week or so of this and you will start mumbling to yourself, or worse, just moving your lips as you gaze for a long time at your next door neighbor hosing down his driveway, even though it's raining. He, too, is retired and has joined a support group. He continues to hose down his driveway for most of the morning. He is waiting for the water to stop because he has forgotten how to turn off the tap. You go over to help and find that you have also forgotten. Later when both of you realize it isn't going to stop, you invite him over for a peanut butter sandwich but, after finding the refrigerator, you find that you have forgotten the ingredients. He seems not to care. He's forgotten why he is there, anyway. So have you. You eat a paper napkin. It tastes O.K. so you make one for him. One day some nice people call. At first you believe they are sent by the church, but later realize that they are foreign espionage agents. When they attempt to feed you malt extract you bite their fingers. They never come back and you write a long, rambling letter to the newspaper, in crayon. When the letter isn't published you fly into a tantrum and throw your morning porridge at the postman. In so doing you fall off the porch and break your hip

    After you leave hospital you hop around the porch shouting at people on the street. When someone shouts back you swear and shake your crutch in the air. After you leave the hospital again, you discover that you are now known as "That Crazy Old Bastard on Maple." Young children tell stories about how you live in a cellar with giant rats and how you cooked and ate your whole family but were found not guilty on account of being insane at the time. They dare each other to ring your doorbell and a particularly nasty boy with red hair and warts on his knees eggs you when you open the door. One morning you wake to find that it takes eleven minutes to pee. Ten minutes later you have to pee again. All your teeth are starting to wobble and there's a three-inch hair growing out of your nose. Following your shower you cannot hear properly and believe that your head has filled up with steam. Also the room is full of black spots. Later, a doctor who has just graduated from medical school examines you. He shakes his head and tells you to buy a fly swatter. He calls you George. Your name is Kenneth.

Sometime after this you answer a telephone call from a man who calls you Dad. He is very helpful. You send him your life savings for membership in a plan that will make you financially secure until and if you reach the age of one hundred and ten. He is very sincere. He never phones back and you realize vaguely that you are going to die poor and unwashed. For some strange reason this doesn't bother you too much and you start whistling old Glen Miller tunes, a difficult feat what with the loose teeth and all. One day you pick up a newspaper and read your obituary. Proudly, you point this out but nobody seems to be around or interested. Don't be upset; you can tell them all about it later.

FRACTURED FABLES

Off The Wall

A Historically Incorrect Incident

T he northern reaches of Britain, 180 A.D. It is close to the end of winter, gray, wet and wind swept (as usual). A squad of foot soldiers under the command of Centurian Lucius Crassus is engaged in maintaining a section of Hadrian's Wall. Built as a fortification against marauding tribes the wall so far has done little other than keep out marauding sheep or the odd wandering Pict. The lads assigned to defend the wall are not a happy lot. Five years in this distant corner of the Roman Empire is not their idea of life in the modern army and serious muttering has begun. The best trained mutterer among them is Appius Tullius, a legal scribe before enlisting. Appius, refused promotion for trying to start a foot soldier's union, is something of a barrack room lawyer. He speaks with heavy disgust.

Appius: "Be the best you can be" they said. "See the world and serve your emperor," they said. And what did we get? Five years in this arse-end country, half of them doing pick and shovel up here. It might have escaped your notice but we should have been rotated two years ago.

Several of his comrades nod but look about uneasily. Centurion Crassus has sharp ears and is well known for his zero tolerance on muttering. Appius, unmindful of their nervousness, continues.

Appius: (bitterly) We're growing old up here. Gaius, there - as fine a head of hair as I ever saw and look at him now. Bald as an egg!"

Gais: (embarrassed) It's prob'ly the rain. They say it gets in at the roots.

Appius: It's creepin' old age, mate, is what it is. And look at Junius. What sort of a life is this for a young fellow like him, eh? He doesn't know what it's for apart from makin' a puddle, does 'e?

Junius: (indignantly) Of course I do! I've been to Londinium, once and...

Appius: (wistfully) Aye, lad! We've all been to Londinium...Cor!

As they continue discussing their miserable lot, Centurion Crassus rides up rather tiredly, followed by his cohort sergeant, Brutus Collatinus (known behind his back as Gluteus Maximus). Brutus is a twenty-year regular with a flattened nose and small red eyes. He has recently lost a month's pay casting dice in the N.C.O's Club and is in no mood to humor anybody. He communicates in that shrieking falsetto so beloved of sergeants throughout history.

Brutus: 'ello-'ello-'ello! What's all this 'ere, then, you 'orrible little men? Doubling on the spot...wait for it, wait for it - Double! - Get them knees up, get them knees up! Get them knees up!

Crassus, who is recovering from a night's heavy drinking in the commissioned officer's mess, winces painfully.

Crassus: (flicking his riding switch) At ease, at ease! Carry

on sergeant, and for God's sake STOP SHOUT-
ING!

Brutus: (shouting even louder) Right then, you lot! You'll be 'appy to know we're leaving 'ere, tomorra. (He permits them to cheer for a few seconds). But you'll be very un'appy to know where to. (The cheering fades) Ho, yus, my lads very unhappy, I'm 'appy to say.

Crassus: (impatiently) Do get on with it, Sergent.

Brutus: Yessir! So listen up you lot. Who's the clever clogs in this outfit? (he looks at Appius) You, lad, you went to school, tell 'em abaht them Vizzwhats...go on!

Crassus: (yawning) The sergeant's referring to the Visigoths.

Appius: Oh, that lot - a bunch of hairy buggers over in Gaul, I've heard.

Brutus: And you've 'eard right, my old son. Six foot an' up and them's the small ones. Bloody great axes and eat babies for breakfast. A right buncha bastards!

Appius: I take it we're posted to Gaul.

Brutus: (maliciously) There you go! I knew you was a clever clogs. Chance of a lifetime for a fella like you.

Crassus: Well, that will be all, Sergeant.

Brutus: Yessir. Now then, you lucky lads. You 'eard. Pack up your picks an' shovels. We're orf on 'olidays again.

Silently, at first, the lads pack up their kit, then one starts to hum a popular tune. Gradually, the rest join in and soon they start to sing. It is a song well known to soldiers and concerns the personal parts of sergeants and what should be done with them. Gaul, is it? At least it's warmer down there, isn't it? And anywhere's better than here - in the wet; in the cold; in the wind; on the Wall...

FRACTURED FABLES

Yonder Peasant

The winter retreat of Wenceslas, Prince Duke of Bohemia. It is a drear and drafty pile, even by the standards of the day, consisting of a rush-lit dining hall redolent of mice and mildew, a dark, low-beamed kitchen rank with the odor of hung game, a regal bedchamber the canopy of which consists of a drooping and fly-blown tapestry which leaks in wet weather as the roof above is in terminal disrepair. A mildewed dungeon doubles as a guestroom for his unwelcome in-laws who rarely visit and none of whom has ever stayed overnight. The retreat broods over a depressing vista of dwarf scrubs beyond which stagger the remnants of a dilapidated fence defaced by the rustic obscenities of local oafs. As the place is quite remote and Wenceslas something of a recluse, much has passed him by. He knows little of current events and has read nothing of foreign affairs. Now, approaching dotage (possibly something worse) he stands at his bedroom window peering with suspicious eyes over the moonlit winter fields which are now deep in snow. Dimly, his attention is caught by the sight of a lurching figure. Who, or whatever can it be? Reaching for a moldering bell cord he tugs it rather petulantly. Several minutes later his page enters, yawning and snuffling. He is a callow not-to-say surly young lout from the rough end of Prague whence he has fled to evade a morals charge. He is destined to be the last page in the book. (groan)

Wenceslas: (broodingly) God's Wounds! Who is that fellow on my lands? And what's he doing? There's quite a frost out there tonight and perchance the wretch is rabid, God forbid!

Page: (blowing his nose on his nightshirt) What is it now? It's after midnight and I've caught a bleedin' cold, 'aven't I?

FRACTURED FABLES

Wenceslas: I'm sorry, lad but it's that time of year. I have to ask you the questions.

Page: (becoming even more aggressive) You mean that bleedin' carol I suppose. Why don't you give it up? I need my kip.

Wenceslas: Would that I could, lad; would that I could! But tradition demands.

Page: Well, it would, wouldn't it? It comes wiv you bein' a king an' all, don't it?

Wenceslas: (resting a discreet hand on his page's knee and pointing to the window) Hither page, come stand by me, if thou knowest its telling. Yonder peasant, who is he? Where and what his dwelling?

Page: (scornfully) You know who he is - same as last year, an' every one before - a scrubby old duff full of fleas an' worse what lives a good league 'ence, down at the fence, by Saint-who's-er-face's fountain.

Wenceslas: (reprovingly) Come, come, now lad! You mean Saint Agnes, poor thing.

Page: (shrugging) Whatever.

Wenceslas: I wonder what he's doing this time?

Page: What you fink 'es doin'- pickin' bleedin' daisies? Nickin' firewood is what e's doin'. Same as last year an' every other one. I'd 'ave the bugger topped if I was you.

Wenceslas: What matters if he's after a few sticks? Perchance he's in sore need.

Page: He'll rob you blind and come back for more. You won't 'ave a stick left on the hill. I'll give 'im a thump if you want me to.

Wenceslas: But it's the Feast of Stephen. Why don't we have him in and share a pastry or two while he warms his bottom by the fire?

Page: (shivering) I wouldn't say no to a bit of warm meself. It's cold as a gravedigger's arse in here.

Wenceslas: It's in The Carol, isn't it? 'Bring me flesh and bring me wine, bring me pine logs hither, thou and I shall see him dine...' and, er, etcetera...Oh, dear, I seem to have forgotten the rest...

Page: It seems to me you've forgot a lot of fings. Like last time f'rinstance...

Wenceslas: I don't recall... I don't recall...

Page: Well, I do, mate - same old duff, on the scrounge. You wasn't so generous then. You threw a fit and had him thrashed around the yard, then set the 'ounds on him. I can see it now! 'im 'oppin all over the yard an' yellin' 'is bleedin' 'ead off, two dogs 'angin' from his arse. Talk about a lark! I never seen a peasant move so smart!

Wenceslas: (bewildered) I don't recall... I don't recall...I don't...

FRACTURED FABLES

~~~~~~

Oop At Fahrm

Introduction: A domestic drama in the vernacular of northern moorland English - a not-altogether easy assay as dialects vary from parish to parish even within contiguous districts. Prepare, then, to struggle and strive. Good luck!

A wind-scoured prospect of dales, becks and fells. It is high summer in Bronte country where it has been raining steadily for three months or so. A dank, smothering fog lies over everything; air and earth are saturated. A few drenched sheep stand in the foreground bleating dismally. Tourists are objects of wonder and suspicion. Ahead, on a rise of land, the vague and gaunt outline of a gray stone building can be seen faintly between the pelting squalls. This is Baldrock Farm, a two-hundred and fifty-years old wreck with many bricked-up window arches and several collapsed chimneys, the roof slates buried beneath thick layers of moss and crow lime. Situated at the end of a churned and rutted track, it is the ancestral home of Alfred Umbrage, his unfortunate heirs and assigns. Umbrage is a powerful, blunt-jawed patriarch in his late sixties given to intemperate opinions and choleric outbursts. As we join him he is sitting impatiently at table in the large, drafty kitchen, knife and fork grasped vertically in great, raw-knuckled hands. He is waiting for his wife, Doris, a marginally younger woman, to serve him his dinner. Tonight, it is the usual — a thick slab of roast beef, a puffed Yorkshire pudding large enough to choke a cart horse, a mound of mashed turnips, and a whole head of cabbage. Warming on the hearthstone is a gray, Spotted-Dick Dumpling and a jug of thick custard. Accompanied by copious drafts of peat-colored tea, this has been standard fare for as long as memory serves. Umbrage belches explosively and prods the beef with his fork. "Give us a borrow of thy teeth, Missus," he demands.

This transaction effected, Umbrage chomps and

gasps through his simple repast in stolid, workmanlike fashion. Finished, he reaches for the gravy jug and pouring what's left down his throat he belches powerfully, returns the borrowed dentistry to Doris before crossing to the settle upon which he lowers his dung-encrusted corduroys. Wind howls in fitful gusts about the eaves and in the chimney causing slates to rattle down the roof and sulphurous billows of smoke to fume the kitchen. Thus ensconced, Umbrage holds forth: "Ah towd oud Tom to shut top field gate, and what does 'e do? Leaves it off t'hook, that's what 'e does, the bloody owd fool? Theer's a randy young stirk up in top corner as'll 'ave a go at out as moves. It's gettin' 'igh time 'e went to t'knacker yard if thou wants my opinion!"

Doris sluices her recovered dentistry under the kitchen tap then fits them back in her mouth. "T'knacker yard? Thou must be daft, mister! Yon bullock's only two years old."

Umbrage looks up over his mug of tea. "Don't be so bloody daft thy sen! Ah'm talkin' about owd Tom, not young bullock. Now pass ower t'paper, ah need to catch up."

Thus, seated by the fire, his socks steaming rankly, Umbrage scrutinizes The Crag and Croft Clarion. He is not impressed with what he reads. "Well, I'll be buggered! Just listen to this!" His neck ripely mottled, he holds forth: "Ah, never heard such a load of owd tripe!" He tilts back his head, adjusts his wire-framed glasses and reads aloud: "'T'district Council met on fust of t'month an' voted unanimous for street lamps in Ullage.'" He glowers around. "Theer's only 'alf a dozen folks down theer an' they're all daft as barnyard brushes! Street lamps in Ullage while us up 'ere 'ave to manage wi' lanterns. By gum, missus, Council must 'ave gone mental"

Doris scrapes the last of the custard into a slop pail and gives her considered opinion. "Thou'ld only complain if we 'ad 'em up 'ere. Besides, light from t'lanterns is cosy I'd say."

Umbrage shuffles the sheets in search of something else to attack. Finding another item worthy of his ire, he launches forth: "Now, this is ripe!" He quotes: "'Three-'eaded calf born on local fahrm. Man from t'Ministry studying t'matter.'" He continues his harangue.

"That'll be some stuck-up bugger from t'city I don't doubt. Weekend farmer like as not who doesn't know a cow's 'ead from a donkey's arse."

Doris starts to poke down the kitchen fire. "Thou should be more broad-minded, I'd say."

Umbrage turns a few more pages but finding nothing else to grieve throws the newspaper onto the dying fire. "I've a mind to write a line or two except I dropped my pen in t'pigstye." He continues to brood until a new thought strikes him. "What's 'is lordship up to these days?"

Doris considers an answer to this. "T'lad, thou means?"

"Aye, 'im. Who else? 'e 'asn't written nigh on."

Doris scrapes the dinner leavings into a bucket under the sink. "'appen 'e's busy wi' summat or t'other."

Umbrage considers this information. "Busy? 'im? What at?"

"Well, readin' 'istory last time 'e called."

"'istory? What bloody 'istory?"

"Renaissance 'istory."

"What kind of 'istory is that? 'istory's all finished now. 'e should be 'ere, on t'fahrm wi' us muckin' out beasts, not buggerin' about wi' what's-it-called 'istory."

Doris bristles. "Theer's more to life, mister, than barnyard an' t'beasts."

Umbrage protests. "Barnyard an' beasts 'as kept us in bread, sup an' all. An' I know nowt about owt, I suppose."

"Thou said it, father."

"Well, if that's thy tune I'm off up stairs."

"Thou can suit thyself."

Umbrage stops with one foot on the bottom step. "By gum, Missus, an' don't think I won't, neither! To think I've a son as 'as turned against family an' t'fahrm, rain an' wind an' snow in winter! An' t'smell of beasts as well I'll be bound."

Doris damps down the fire with the last of the tea. "Well, I'm glad thou likes summut as 'appens."

Umbrage stands with a foot on the stairs. "Like it? Like what? Thou must think I've gone fond! Ah bloody well 'ates it up 'ere...!"

FRACTURED FABLES

The Three Bean Scam

Adventures in The Used-Cow Trade

Long, long ago there lived a poor widow woman with her accidental son Jack. One day when the widow was poorer than usual, having spent all her housekeeping money on home-brewed stout and nettle beer, she hiccupped at Jack, "Get off your bottom and go sell Old Bossie."

"Sell who?" asked Jack, who rarely heard things right the first time round due to cumulative clouts upon his ears.

"Old Bossie," his mother said darkly. "What else can I sell?"

"Why don't we sell her milk instead, mother?" Jack

asked as he had a great fondness for the beast.

"Because she's been dry for three years now," his mother snapped.

"Then what have I been drinking for breakfast mother?"

"You don't want to know," the widow said shortly. "Now get on your way and don't dare bring her back."

Reluctantly, Jack put a dry cheese rind in his pocket and led Old Bossie off through the woods. As he approached his destination his nose told him that it was market day. Perhaps he could make an early sale, get back in time for supper and his mother would cook him some gruel. Jack's footsteps quickened.

Arrived at the market place Jack found it crowded with beet-faced farmers waving sticks and swearing loudly. Nobody gave Old Bossie a glance. This was hardly to be wondered at as she had but one eye and smelled quite badly. All day Jack stood in the market square and watched while the farmers cursed each other and prodded their cattle, after which they went to the village inn and spent all their profits on cider and trollops. What a fine, fresh-air life Jack thought in envy. If only he could grow up quickly and be just like them.

When the market closed, Jack headed back through the woods towards home. What would the widow say when she learned he had not sold Old Bossie? Having a keen sense of history he preferred not to dwell on it. Already the sun was low in the sky and in the gathering gloom beneath the trees strange shadows formed. He was half way through the woods when one of the shadows jumped out before him. It was a small, dapper man in snappy, town suiting who popped his thumbs nimbly and whistled a jig. "Good evening, young fellow," the little man said.

"Good evening to you, sir," responded Jack courteously, for although he knew little of life he was of a mannerly disposition.

The little man eyed Jack merrily. "Tell me," he said, "What's a young lad like you doing out in these parts?"

"I'm back from the market with Bossie unsold, and I fear my mother will thrash me again."

The little man screwed up his face in sympathy. "Ah, now, is that the way of it, then?" he mused. "So I'll tell you what I'll do for you. Why don't you sell Old Bossie to me? Then when you get home you'll get kisses, not clouts."

"Oh, thank you, sir," said Jack, his future brightening considerably. "How much will you give me for this fine beast?"

The little man looked at the cow with distaste. He plucked his lip then shook his head sadly. "I never saw a cow so sorry. She's good for little other than dog food or glue."

"Oh, dear," whined Jack, his hopes on the wane.

"Now don't take on, so, Jack," the little man said. "Wait 'til I tell you what I'll do."

Jack looked doubtful. "How did you know my name is Jack?"

"Flute! I didn't at all. It's just that I call everyone Jack. A common and popular name so it is."

"Well, how much will you give me for Old Bossie, then?"

"Jack, I kid you not. Twenty years in the business and I've never seen worse. But I fancy your face so here's what I'll do. She isn't worth beans, but that's what I'll give you."

"Just beans!" Jack protested.

"Trust me," the little man said. Have I ever lied to you before?"

"No," Jack said. You haven't ever seen me before." The little man popped his fingers one-two-three. "Then there you go, Jack!" he said and flipped three beans into Jack's shirt pocket.

"Three beans!" said Jack. The mum will skin me!"

But the little man had jumped back into a nearby shadow. Jack was alone in the gathering dark. How had he been so easily tricked? And what would he say to his mother? Not knowing what to do, Jack took the three beans out of his pocket. They weren't too impressive and certainly not worth having in place of Old Bossie, her smell notwithstanding. But suddenly a story came into his mind. Something about three magic beans and a mile-high beanstalk? And wasn't there gold at the top? Perhaps his mother would get all excited and forget to thrash him. At least he could tell her the story. What other options did he have?

Jack wended his way back through the darkened forest until he saw the light of his home. Approaching the door he paused and reflected. Perhaps he could get through his bedroom window and not get thrashed until morning. But as he crept up to the cottage his mother called out. "Is that you, our Jack?"

Jack knew from her voice she was not feeling festive. Trembling, he lifted the latch and entered. Inside, his mother was taking her three-monthly bath.

"So what did you get for old Bossie?" she asked.

"No money, mother. No one would buy." Jack said.

"Wouldn't buy!" the widow said ominously. "You mean you didn't sell?"

Jack told her about his long stand in the market, and the red-faced shouting farmers who wouldn't even look at Old Bossie even when they got all cross-eyed and drunk. And he told her about his meeting with the smart little man in the forest and held out the beans in his hand.

"What!" snapped his mother, "You took beans for Bossie!" and without warning she flung the bar of hard yellow soap with which she had been scraping herself. As usual the widow's aim was unerring.

"But, mother," Jack said as his nose swelled up, "suppose they really are magical beans?"

The widow snatched the beans from Jack's open hand and flung them through the broken window. "Magic beans! They're just jelly beans!"

Later, his ears boxed purple, Jack climbed the ladder up to the loft which he shared with an owl and his mother's stale empties, then lying back on an old grain sack, he cried himself to sleep.

In gray dawn light Jack woke and stared at the broken rafters above. Then he remembered the day before. Seized with hope, he ran to the window and peered down into the garden. Nothing at all. No beanstalk growing up to the sky; no mystic castle among the clouds; no gold for the taking. The widow was right; the beans were just beans. Dimly, Jack saw that he had been hornswoggled, a word he'd often wondered about but was unable to spell or pronounce. As he struggled with this dismal fact, he heard the first cork pop. The widow was starting early today. Jack sighed. Why couldn't he have been born someone else? Perhaps Dick Whittington, become Mayor of London, had his mother committed and lived happily ever after? He struggled for a word to describe his situation but couldn't seem to find one. Then suddenly he had an insight - Bummer. All he needed to do was add an exclamation mark.

FRACTURED FABLES

The Lonely Grave Of Granny McDuff

(Oh, Canada!)

Writers who are infected with the expectation of actually earning something for their midnight sweat other than hoots of derision are often attracted by the prizes offered in the National Short Story/Personal Essay type contests. These periodic events inflame the imagination of literary aspirants from coast to coast. Based on the assumption that anyone capable of putting together a string of understandable sentences must have something worthwhile writing about, these contests are made the more attractive by prizes of real money. Writers, even regularly published ones, are always excited by the prospect of actually being paid. It's not just the confirmation that they have mastered the complications of their craft, or that they have written something others are willing to read: it's the actual cash.

Asked by an aspirant what was the key to being favorably considered in this type of contest I offered the following:

Leverage: You must have leverage. And the way to acquire leverage depends upon some well established principles. Thus, it will avail the aspirant writer nothing if he or she ignores some very basic rules and requirements. Take by way of example the biographic essay. Here mortality is paramount. Pick a dead subject rather than a live one as they cannot contradict you. Do a relative in preference to any other provided they did or said something meaningful of record. This gives you the inside track and saves time researching the lives of strangers. Make sure the relative has been dead long enough for surviving family members to have received all posthumous left-overs and to have lost interest in what you will claim the deceased said or did. For instance your maternal great grandmother might be good material. (Can. Lit. is stiff with dead great grandmothers). So, having decided, consider carefully. Was Granny McDuff of the right material? That is, does she, postmortem, come up to snuff? Was she, for example, properly born in some moose-haunted pasture on the Canadian Shield? Was she brought up surrounded by bush and ravaged by blackflies? Did she regale her kin and anyone else within earshot with such pithy aphorisms as "It was so cold in the winter the lanterns froze solid."

Never omit such telling facts as the methods used by Granny McDuff in the making of her own laundry soap from bird lime and hog fat. Don't forget the daily three-mile, mosquito-plagued trudge to the creek for drinking water. Tell also how she got by on four hours sleep, having to sit up half the night sewing turnip sacks into curtains and long johns by the light of a guttering candle. Mention, too, that she always addressed her husband as "Mister" McDuff and that she survived him by twenty-five years. Such revelations inspire deep pride and emotion within the native breast.

Be sure to inform everyone that Granny McDuff

had no interest in 'politicking' or 'man talk.' Refer to her as 'a tower of strength in times of adversity.' Describe her as being 'straight as a lodgepole and hard as hickory.' Invest her with eyes that 'though faded by time, still retained their piercing directness.' Make her a little eccentric. No full-blown mania, but just a touch odd, terse in speech, outspoken in opinion, an ardent admirer of Sir John A. McDonald and, though opposed to strong drink in public, was not above taking a wee nip at home. In short, describe her as the sort of relative no one of sound mind would want to meet more than once in a lifetime.

Do all these things and you will have created "an unforgettable character of profound humanness, embodying those traditional and unshakeable virtues that laid the very foundations of our pioneer heritage."

Finally, and this is paramount to your essay, NEVER FORGET TO MENTION THE GRAVE. The grave is pivotal and should adhere to strict and time-honored specifics. It must be located near a solitary pine in some bleak and forgotten corner, and lie beneath a headstone of weather-worn Cambrian granite surrounded by dry tamarack shrubs through which the wind whistles plaintively all year round. Don't overdo the scene: a crow or two flapping overhead, perhaps. Mention a few distant strains from a north country fiddle. And one final touch — remember to give the headstone a tilt. At two thousand words Old Granny should fetch First Prize!

about the author...

Joe Roland, retired feature columnist with the Vancouver Courier, kept his readers entertained or infuriated for many years with his witty takes on everyday life. Born in Staffordshire, England, he served in the RAF and worked as a forester, a librarian and an advertising copywriter before emigrating to Canada. In Toronto he worked as a patent writer then joined the CBC as a film editor. His travels took him to the West Coast where he eventually settled and took up freelance journalism. He currently lives in Tsawwassen, British Columbia with his wife Helen who corrects his spelling and censors unacceptable words.

© 2012 Joe Roland
All rights reserved
Published by Caldron Books
Vancouver, Canada

ISBN 978-0-9878612-0-7 (pbk.)
ISBN 978-0-9878612-1-4 (ebk.)

Book design by Footeprint Communications

www.ingramcontent.com/pod-product-compliance
Lightning Source LLC
Chambersburg PA
CBHW061653040426
42446CB00010B/1722